CW00375421

THE ART OF
NEGOTIATION

HOW TO GET
WHAT YOU WANT
(EVERY TIME)

TIM CASTLE

I AM SELF-PUBLISHING

@iamselfpub
www.iamselfpublishing.com

Dedicated to Sandra and Levi –
my everything

CONTENTS

INTRODUCTION

What Improving Your Negotiation Skills Can Do For You

NEGOTIATION PLAYS A big part in our everyday life. Whether we like it or not, we are all involved in negotiation at some point in our lives. It may be buying our dream house or landing the next promotion at work; negotiation and how we approach it has a major effect on the outcome. The fact is, improving your negotiation skills is not only lucrative, it's also essential.

The world is moving at such a rapid pace that you need to understand how to negotiate in a variety of different contexts, mediums and timescales. For instance, problem solving. This skill, which is strongly linked to negotiation principles, was ranked at number 12 in the Fortune 500 most valued characteristics of an employee back in 1970; and is now sitting at number 2 in 2017.

Today, negotiation reigns supreme as one of the most valued skills that employers look for. We live in a fast-paced, digitally savvy, uber-connected world, so it's even more important to be equipped with the skills that you need to set yourself up for success. Whether you are an experienced negotiator or new to negotiation, my goal is to give you some new perspectives and strategies on negotiation, as well as techniques to practise for the long term, so that you are set up to achieve even more from your negotiations.

Over the course of this book, I will show you how to master all of the elements that make up successful negotiation. You might be wondering, if this is so important to my success, why have I not heard about it before? Well, there are 3 reasons:

1. The truth is that negotiation is talked about; but just not widely taught. It's deemed to be a skill that you pick up along the way through experience, rather than one that can be taught in a classroom.
2. Not everyone is good at negotiation or even likes it for that matter; therefore, they tend to shy away from it. If you're a business leader who hates to negotiate, you will most likely outsource it and employ someone to negotiate on your behalf.
3. It can sometimes be hard for leaders to promote a topic that they know little about. The truth is, advanced competency in negotiation will set you apart from the rest. Not only will it give you an edge professionally, but it will also pay dividends in your personal life too.

Once you realise that 'it is possible', you will experience more success than you ever thought was available before, and the knock-on effect will be that you expect the best in every situation and, therefore, understand the variety of options available to you. On top of this, you will also see your creativity and persistence increase through practising successful negotiation. Tony Robbins, the world-famous expert in self-development, repeatedly talks about this. He calls it the belief, potential, action and results quadrant. The cycle works like this: the more you believe something is possible, the more potential you see, and because you think it has potential, you undertake the massive action that is required to achieve the goal and produce the result. This, in turn, becomes a self-fulfilling prophecy. As you experience more and more success and take the necessary action to achieve the results that you want, your confidence and self-belief increases, the actions you take increase and so the cycle continues, bringing you ever-increasing levels of success.

We'll explore this phenomenon and others in the chapters ahead in this book but what is important to get at this stage is the specific strategies, tools and beliefs you will need to adopt to set yourself up for world-class negotiation success.

Gaining competence in negotiation when you are under pressure and the stakes are high will open the door to a new world of possibility, not only in your personal life, but in business too. The ability to negotiate has never been more important, and this book is for anyone who is looking to get more confident at negotiations and is committed to the process of growing this area of their life. It doesn't matter what background, culture or walk of life you come from, we all face negotiations in our lives and I want to share this manual with you in the hope that it will allow you to have more success.

The likes of Sir Richard Branson, Elon Musk, Jeff Bezos, Steve Jobs, Larry Page, Sergey Brin, Arianna Huffington, Barack Obama, Michael Jordan and Beyoncé all use negotiation to make their dreams come true and ensure their future success. Isn't it about time you did the same?

You could be a builder, lawyer, nurse, accountant, hairdresser, homeless person, pilot or gardener or be travelling or unemployed. You could be many things. The point is, it doesn't matter; negotiation will affect you in some way, shape or form. This book is for you.

Your journey as a negotiator begins today, with you picking up this book and deciding to learn more about negotiation techniques for successful outcomes. It's important to get to grips with the concepts and see how they are playing out in your life today. I am not all-knowing, I just want to share with you my perspective on negotiation and provide you with some key skills to practise that will help you have more successful negotiations in your life.

How I learned to negotiate

I was just like you, I know exactly how it feels to stand in your shoes and be intimidated by negotiation. I wasn't born with this gift – I've learned my craft, and as a result have lived and breathed negotiation in both my personal and professional life over the past 12 years. Upon graduating from university with a degree in psychology, I joined the UK's largest media barter agency and began negotiating for a living. Essentially, media barter allows companies to part pay for their advertising and increase marketing budgets by using their own products. For example, BMW may have a whole airfield full of cars just sitting their ready to go, waiting to be sold. However, the company may not have the marketing budget for the campaign it wants to run. This presents an opportunity, as they can unlock the value of the cars and achieve their marketing goals by leveraging a media barter agency to negotiate exchanging their unsold cars for the advertising campaign they need. Like negotiation, bartering has been around since the dawn of time, helping businesses to overcome obstacles and solve problems by thinking about things from another perspective. I learned on the job here, negotiating multimillion pound deals in the day and building valued relationships at night. Negotiating became part of my life on a personal and professional level, but there was one life-changing incident back when I was only 20 that really kick-started my negotiation skills. This experience fundamentally transformed how I understood what was possible in life through the power of negotiation.

It was make or break and I was faced with my own real negotiation situation when it really mattered.

Right after my first year of university, I got a job as a downhill mountain bike instructor at a US summer camp in the Pennsylvania mountains. It was only supposed to be for six weeks but I ended up staying stateside for a year. When I returned to Northumbria University in Newcastle a year later, sporting a healthy tan and blond dreadlocks that grew way past my shoulders, everything had changed. My classmates had moved on into the third year and had new friends, so overall the place wasn't the same for me as it had been in my first year. I had changed.

As a result of travelling back and forth travel from the States a lot, I'd been spending more and more time in London, and so I decided after a week back in Newcastle that my only option was to transfer to Goldsmiths College, University of London. I'm not sure if I realised it then, but giving myself one shot and narrowing my options like this meant that I focused completely on the task at hand. I was all in. Looking back on the experience now, with perhaps more of a mature view, I recognise that there were, of course, plenty of other universities that I could have approached. However, having this extreme focus at a time when I was making such a radical change as a young 20-year-old out to prove himself in the world, made all the difference. By committing all the way, I convinced myself that it would happen, which led to a level independent thinking that allowed me to forge the path, no matter what anyone else said. I was also somewhat familiar with Goldsmiths, having previously been on a campus tour a number of years earlier on one of my many expeditions to seek out the very best that the UK had to offer in the way of university experiences.

This decision brought with it a myriad of problems, the first being that the course began in two days and I had just signed a year-long lease on a room in Newcastle. On top of this, in order to have any chance of success and before they could even consider me, I had to officially resign from my current course enrolment.

My second problem was created by my first, by withdrawing from enrolment I was no longer in the Universities and Colleges Administration System (UCAS) and, therefore, didn't have a profile or any formal process for applying. In the UK, UCAS is the organisation that handles applications for potential students seeking to apply for a university place. Without them I was very going against the grain of normal practice. It was effectively like walking into a company without an interview. To make matters worse, when I called Goldsmiths to enquire about the possibility of transferring, they told me I couldn't speak to the course leader (the ultimate decision maker) as he was off sick. In addition, the psychology course had unfortunately already maxed out its intake by six people, so they simply didn't have space, especially for someone who wasn't in the UCAS system.

So what options did I have?

The first thing I did was tell the Goldsmiths receptionist my story; I got her name and started to build the foundation of a relationship with her. Then, every time I rang, I called her by name and made sure she knew my cause. If this was going to happen, I would need her backing as the gatekeeper; I needed her on side to make calls on my behalf and fight my corner internally. One thing I did right from the start was commit. I made my intention clear; I told her it was 'Goldsmiths or nothing'.

Then, I asked her to hypothetically imagine that I was in the UCAS system. What would they require for me to apply for the course; what would I need to do?

She reeled off a list of things I would 'hypothetically' need: a personal statement, a letter from the current dean, a university reference from the lecturer and copies of all my grades. 'Oh and you'll need to be here on Thursday morning for the induction, if you are to have any chance.' It was now Tuesday, and bearing in mind that I had been travelling for a year, I didn't have any of these documents with me; I knew it was time to hustle.

I had 48 hours to turn my situation around and present myself in London for inspection. In this moment, I realised it was crucial to get all the balls in motion one by one, and then keep them moving, without dropping one. I hired a car and enlisted the help of my friend Richard who had come to visit me for the weekend (what a fun weekend for him!).

We packed up all my worldly possessions and I paid the landlady my month's deposit for the inconvenience of breaking the lease and finding a new tenant. You might say to me 'what about the money?' In this situation and at times like these it's important to focus on the bigger picture. When time was my biggest issue, I reasoned that, in the grand scheme of things, spending a day finding a new tenant was less worthwhile than persuading the landlady to break the lease and let me go for a relatively small fee.

What we are talking about is me talking my way into a top London university in just two days with nothing but myself. Part of this negotiation skill is working out what to prioritise. In this case, money was going to be spent. The issue was making sure that I was there, presentable and ready to go in two days' time, and I had everything they needed from me to make it happen.

I called the receptionist every hour to see if she had managed to contact the lecturer; she hadn't. On each call, I made a point of updating her on where I was at, and kept her in the loop so that she felt part of the story. She was now also invested, emotionally, as well as practically through her time. Little by little, rumours of my story started to spread as I kept calling back and more of the office staff got to know me. By this stage they had started rooting for me; a glimmer of hope and possibility had emerged.

Piece by piece, I assembled a makeshift application, and as I signed over my withdrawal from Northumbria University, I knew I was doing the right thing. This was either going to happen or I'd figure it out; I had to try. It had to happen. What I knew was, I had to be in London.

After spending many hours on the phone late into the night and sleeping for only a few hours, I woke up early to pack up my belongings and drive down the length of England to the big smoke. With nothing in the way of an offer letter or formal representation within the UK education system, the one thing I had to do was keep my mind focused on the task at hand.

For these 48 hours, it was crucial that I had my wits about me if I was to convince Goldsmiths to grant me a place. I needed to make it as easy as possible for them to do so and demonstrate that I was committed.

As I waved goodbye to Richard, driving out of Newcastle and across the Tyne Bridge, I began to contemplate the task at hand, so I cranked up Radio One and drove with purpose all the way to London.

After three hours of driving, I called into our home in Ollerton for a pit stop and to see my dad, who I realised hadn't been updated on the new plan. Oops. As I pulled into the driveway, my car full to the brim with all my possessions (electric drum kit, guitar, skateboard), I could see the look of disappointment on Dad's face. He thought I was returning home having packed up and left university for a second time (I had started and dropped out of a chemistry degree at Birmingham University some two years earlier).

Dad came up to the side of the car and said, 'That's it then, you're back,' as I was getting out. I was quick to put him straight, my mind acutely focused on the mission. 'I'm passing through on my way to London; I'm going to get into a London university.'

Dad didn't challenge me or try to put me off. I went out for some lunch with Dad and my sister, and spirits were high, albeit a little confused. I could tell they were wondering if I would pull this off, but I think they could see in my eyes there was no putting me off; the determination was there. I was doing it. I carried on my journey and reached London at sunset. I was tired.

The next morning, I awoke at the crack of dawn, still in communication with the psychology department receptionists. All of them now knew who I was by now. 'I'm here,' I said. 'I've made it to London and will see you at the induction day.'

As I walked into the lecture theatre, people turned and looked; everyone seemed to know my name. Or possibly it was because of the bleach blond dreadlocks down to my shoulders.

As I took my seat a girl with red hair leaned over and said, 'So you're the infamous Tim Castle, are you?' 'That's right,' I replied, 'nice to meet you.' Turns out most of the department had heard of me and my story to get into Goldsmiths.

If I hadn't kept my mindset on track, it wouldn't have happened. I had to believe that it could happen, so numerous others would also believe and connect to my journey.

When I graduated two years later, I was stood on the college green outside the Richard Hoggart Building thanking each of the receptionists who had remembered my entrance into the world of Goldsmiths.

This experience fundamentally changed my understanding of negotiation and what is possible. It also catapulted my negotiation skills to the next level; sometimes when we put it all on the line, and there is no turning back, the experience will motivate us to push past our normal boundaries and open the door to what's possible.

BEFORE WE GET STARTED

'Action is the foundational key to all success.'

Pablo Picasso

BEFORE WE GET started, I wanted to give you a quick overview of the lingo and basic thought processes that top negotiators use, as well as a give you a rundown on how to use this book and get the most out of it.

Some words you need in your negotiating vocabulary

Here are some of the words and phrases that are likely to crop up in a negotiation process, so it's a good idea to familiarise yourself with them now.

Back of an envelope

Wherever you are, the back of a taxi, in a restaurant or at the park, don't be afraid to pull out a napkin or scrap of paper and do a quick calculation to make sure the proposed deal makes sense. Know your boundaries. Know where you need to be, and keep it simple. Have a backup option. For example, if they don't want to do it this way, you have another way of reaching an equally beneficial deal. It will help you to feel more in control and reduce any anxiety.

You want to use whatever you can, in the time that you've got, to create a favourable situation. It's all about creating advantages.

Benchmarks

This one is especially important. Benchmarks or anchor points can find their way into negotiations at any stage, anywhere. It is vital that you are on the lookout for these sneaky suckers, as they cause the negotiation to become hamstrung between an invisible ceiling or a floor.

Benchmarks define the outcome of a negotiation by setting the expectation. For example, if someone says, 'I only have 24 hours to do the deal', 'I can only go as low as $500', 'last time I got a 20% discount' or 'last year we made $400m in profit' these are all benchmarks. They refer to specific situations in specific contexts. Whenever someone brings up historical data, for example last year's revenue, they are benchmarking or anchoring to that point in time, rather than looking at the context of the situation in today's reality. It's an important concept to grasp as it can tie the negotiation to situations, people or places that don't reflect today's world.

Another example is the old menu trick used by restaurants to psychologically produce sales of a specific product through anchoring. Guy Ford, Director of MBA program at University of Sydney's Business School gave us this example in his Financial Management class. A superb class by the way, Guy has an excellent way of bringing finance topics to life and making them relatable, memorable and humorous. The way it works is you put an item on the menu for an incredibility high price (e.g. platter of 12 oysters for $1000) and then directly below, ever so discretely, there's a far more reasonable platter of 12 oysters for $100.

The rational mind sees the $1000 dish and then spots the $100 dish, reasoning now that the $100 plate is indeed a bargain in comparison to the one above. In reality, the $1000 plate is the decoy. It's been placed there to distract you from the $100 plate. The $100 is actually the target and where the restaurant is making a significant margin, but our eyes get drawn to the $1000 plate and it becomes our benchmark. Suddenly, the $100 plate of oysters doesn't seem like such a bad deal. The next time you go to a restaurant, look out for the decoy.

My advice about countering benchmarks comes down to awareness. You must be alert and listen for the benchmarks being set the next time you are in a negotiation. Benchmarks are easy to spot once you listen for them.

For example, sales targets based on the previous year's quarterly revenue. This is an anchor; it's based on the context of last year and not in the present. The same happens in negotiations.

'We usually sell this car for $12k.' *Anchor!*

'These trainers usually sell at $220.' *Anchor!*

'The house next door sold for $1.2m.' *Anchor!*

Remember to look closely at the context of the information and notice if it's in a different time period, season, region or economic period.

The thing to remember in all of this is the world is not a static place; economically our lives are constantly changing. This means there is huge scope for opportunity and as a result of all this flux going on around us, different businesses will face different challenges at different times.

It is the people and businesses who capitalise on this and understand this concept who will do well. People and businesses that resist this changing world and want to continue along the same old path, doing the deals that they've always done, will ultimately fail because they aren't building the broad set of relationships needed to carry them through.

Caveat

A caveat is a certain clause or condition that is applied to the deal. Caveats can be your best friend in negotiation, so pay special attention and be sure to read them carefully; they matter a great deal. They often mean more than the deal itself. Use caveats to your advantage, and make sure that you are covered for a range of different scenarios. You also need to fully understand the other party's caveats; be bold and push for clarity. All too often there is a tendency in the excitement of the deal closing to rush to sign without fully understanding what's at stake and under what exact conditions the deal is being done.

Cents in the dollar

For example, I'll give you 80 cents in the dollar means I'll give you 80% of what it's worth. Written 80c/$.

Commercially beneficial

At some point in the negotiation, we need to ask ourselves: does what's being proposed make sense from a commercial perspective? When I talk about making sense, I mean sense within the context, sense for the long-term and sense for the state of the business. Sometimes, in the excitement of possibility, we can get caught up in the idea, especially with likeable people who have mastered the art of selling. We can start to think that their ideas are our ideas and get caught up in the fun of it. If the deal is commercially beneficial, it offers us real business value that we would struggle to achieve elsewhere and could be considered incremental.

This could be strategic alliances, new business, alternative revenue streams and new relationships.

Deal period

It is incredibly important to clarify upfront the period over which the deal will run; when payments will be collected; at what point the deal will be reviewed; if there are any periods of exclusivity; if there are any 'get out' clauses and, if so, by what date would they need to be activated. Does the deal period run over the financial year, calendar year or is it ad hoc? At what point is the deal up for renewal? Will it go into rolling contract after an initial period?

Ducks in a row

This means getting your facts and information in order. Before you pick up the phone or enter a conversation involving negotiation, make sure that you have all the relevant detail and understand it thoroughly so you can execute. Having your ducks in a row allows you to remain calm while presenting the information and gives you the flexibility to manoeuvre as the negotiation twists and turns, rather than needing to pause the negotiation mid-flow to check facts, cross-check information or get approval.

Let's 'park' it

If the negotiation is getting tense, one way to keep momentum and ensure the deal stays on track is to set aside or 'park' the stickier elements of the deal for discussion at a later point in time.

Rolling contract

This is where the terms, restrictions and penalties of the initial deal period are dissolved and the contact moves onto a rolling basis (weekly, fortnightly, monthly). This offers more flexibility for termination on both sides. A tip for negotiation on flat rental: push for a point when your contract becomes rolling, ongoing, usually with limited clauses and limited restrictions. For example, when the lease on your apartment goes from a one-year lease clause to a two-week rolling contract, meaning that either party can terminate the agreement with two weeks' notice. It provides more flexibility and is often preferable, depending on your situation.

Take it off the table

This means you are removing it from the negotiation.

Tiers

Doing deals that involve tiers is a tidy way to structure an incentive that increases in value as the agreed volume of business gets bigger. It is often associated with revenue tiers and is a simple way to define the course of business over a selected time period for an agreed upon reward. Aka: Trigger deal, Volume deal.

For example:

Spend	Discount
$0–$999,999	0%
$1,000,000–$2,999,999	5%
3,000,000 +	10%

*Notice how the first tier doesn't have an incentive associated with it. Why? The reason is, typically, the goal of a tier deal is to incentivise action towards a certain figure. Therefore, in this example, it could well be the case that historical spend without incentive would typically reach $1m, and so spend above this threshold is incentivised only to encourage growth rather than reward normal behaviour.

In this example, the goal is to get spend between $1m – $3m+. If we had included a discount for spend before $1m, then it might not encourage the behaviour that we want as there is limited scope for improvement.

Where do you need to be to make this work?

This frames the conversation positively and puts the ball in their court. Furthermore, it gets them imagining the possibility of doing a deal and gives you information on how far-off you are.

How to use this book

The book is laid out as a manual to take you through the fundamentals of negotiation, all the way through to specific scenarios. It is to be read in sequence from start to finish; with each chapter building on the concepts of the previous one. This allows you, the reader, to digest and experience more of what the process of negotiation involves in a variety of contexts, and to develop new techniques that open your eyes to the possibilities.

At the end of chapters 3-10, you will find an easily digestible recap in the form of a quick summary. On top of this, you'll also see an activity section for you to complete. The more that you commit to the process of practising successful negotiation on a daily basis and embrace the activities defined in this book, the greater the value you will receive. I recommend that you buy a small notebook to carry with you whilst reading this book. A number of the activities will require you to note down your reflections, observations and thoughts. It is important that you engage fully with this element of the interactive and transformative learning process.

In addition to this, you may find that particular sections of this book really resonate with you. I'd encourage you to pay particular attention to those points, as they are most pertinent to your negotiation style. Awareness of this is paramount if you are to become a successful negotiator. Make it a conscious habit to note down whatever speaks to you. Your negotiation notebook will be a practical and useful resource beyond the teachings of this book.

Each activity has been created with the goal of experiential learning and is absolutely the best way for you to get the most out of this growth journey. You will also find on page 289 a resources section full of links to a selection of inspiring and noteworthy videos, TED talks and material referred to in the text for you to review at your leisure.

Above all else, if you only remember one thing from this book, remember this: negotiation is supposed to be fun, and the journey laid out ahead of you as you go through the book has been designed with that same ethos in mind.

This book is meant to be dipped into as part of your morning routine or enjoyed with a glass of wine as a nightly retreat. What's important is that you stick at it and make a habit of working your way through one chapter at a time, whilst completing the activities in the real world and improving your negotiations through practical application.

By the end of the book, you will understand the fundamental principles of negotiation, the various negotiation styles and tactics, and how to avoid the pitfalls. You will also have gained increased competence in structuring the right questions, making requests and, of course, getting the appropriate deal across the line.

So, if you follow the principles set out in this book and you are committed to consistently making successful negotiation a part of your daily routine, you will experience many times over what others have experienced: confidence in negotiating.

PART 1

NEGOTIATION BASICS

1

NEGOTIATION 101

'Human behaviour flows from three main sources:
desire, emotion and knowledge.'

Plato

1.1 What is Negotiation?

HOLLYWOOD WOULD HAVE us believe that all negotiations are the process of a struggle, which occur between two high and mighty CEOs at the top floor of some architecturally impressive skyscraper with an expansive view that spans the breadth of New York City at night, culminating in a boardroom showdown. However, in reality, negotiation can take many forms. Like a chameleon, negotiations can take place in all manner of settings and remain disguised, sometimes only revealing themselves as negotiations at the final stages. It's important to recognise what image negotiation conjures up for you.

Reflect on this for a second; what does negotiation bring up for you?

Negotiation means different things to different people and because it is used in a wide variety of contexts across the globe, we need to take our time to learn and train for these different settings and experiences. From the flea markets of Anjuna, India, haggling for fine silks and wooden carvings, to the launch site of Elon Musk's Space X Falcon 1 rocket, where NASA agreed a $1.5 billion contract, negotiation is taking place.

1.2 What Do We Know About Negotiation Already?

- It is not restricted by boarders or cultures
- It can take different forms
- It can look different in different contexts
- It is important to your success and well-being
- It has been around for centuries and has a direct impact on your success
- It is strongly linked to your beliefs

Definition

In her book, *The Mind and Heart of a Negotiator*, Leigh Thompson refers to negotiation as an 'interpersonal decision-making process' that is 'necessary whenever we cannot achieve our objectives single-handedly'. Thompson is an expert in negotiation and the J Jay Gerber Professor of Dispute Resolution & Organizations in the Kellogg School of Management at Northwestern university, Chicago, Illinois.

However, I would like to go one stage further. I define negotiation as the process of reaching a beneficial agreement that nourishes long-term relationships, wealth and business. It can take many forms, occurring in many places and contexts and is not a mutually exclusive event.

Frameworks

When considering the building blocks of successful negotiation, Harvard Negotiation Project members developed a
framework that provides a clear outline of the core building
blocks of negotiation. The Seven Elements of Effective Negotiation framework are as follows:

1. Interests (collectively articulate and identify
   interests, probe underlying interests)
2. Legitimacy (use external criteria to legitimatise your
   preferred options)
3. Relationships (trustworthy, unconditional, constructive, respectful)
4. Alternatives (identify your best alternative to a
   negotiated agreement)
5. Options (create options to meet the interests of
   both parties)
6. Commitments (plan the time frames, get commitment at the end, not the beginning)
7. Communication (active listening, listen to understand, speak to be understood)

Understanding and acting upon each one of these seven
building blocks, helps us to negotiate more effectively. For
example, by seeking to understand the underlying motivations of our counterpart (Interests), it helps us to put forward
fair and equitable proposals (Legitimacy) without making
silent assumptions that we know what they want (Communication). It is my belief that communication is more than a
fundamental building block and wraps the negotiation from
start through to completion. We will, therefore, delve into
communication tactics in great detail at many points in this
book. It would seem that the project members also agree, as
the framework expands on communication to explicitly state
that its purpose performs two roles. These are:

1. Communicating to gather information – this occurs through core skills, like probing and clarifying. The goal here should be to identify the other party's interests with empathetic questions, such as: "Can you tell me more about…?" and through consequential questioning styles like: "What would you do in the event of…?"
2. Integrative framing styles – paraphrasing and active listening to what the other party has stated to me, including their concerns. This demonstrates respect and builds a connection. Summarising the discussion at the end of each talking point helps to warp up each section of the negotiation and ensures that everyone is singing from the same hymn sheet.

1.3 Negotiation Theories Explained

Distributive vs. integrative

Let's hit the books for a second. Negotiation Theory states there are two types of negotiation:

1. *Distributive*, which is focused on taking as much of a share as possible.
2. *Integrative*, which stems from the principles of co-operation, problem solving and collaboration.

Both negotiation types are used in different contexts. A distributive negotiation could be a case of haggling over the price of a car where there is less interest in forming a relationship or creating a positive impression. In distributive negotiation, there is a tendency to withhold information. For example, you wouldn't want a car salesperson to know how badly you need that car or how much you are really willing to pay for it. Distributive negotiation is short-term focused and centred around 'what's in it for me?' It has the core purpose of extracting the maximum piece of the pie available from the deal.

It is "a winner takes all" strategy and the problem with this type of negotiation mindset is that it fails to recognise that better deals can be created, brokered and agreed upon when there is a valued relationship. The valued relationship facilitates an environment where a level of trust can be established between both parties and, therefore, increased information sharing and collaboration is experienced.

It's my belief that you should be acutely aware of the type of negotiation you are going into and that, broadly speaking, distributive negotiation is not necessarily a type of successful negotiation. Imagine you have been negotiating the price of a car in a distributive fashion with the car salesperson. In this example, you haven't spent time creating a positive impression and you haven't attempted to form any type of relationship. Then you go into work on Monday morning pleased with the sweet deal that you negotiated at the weekend on your car. You smashed that guy on the price; he had nowhere to go and you are feeling like a boss. Then you're called into a meeting and tasked with negotiating the company's corporate fleet of vehicles at that very same garage, with that car salesperson. How much better would it have been to have had an integrative negotiation with the car salesperson now? How much of a better deal could you have reached if you had formed a relationship? By entering every negotiation with an integrative mindset, we set ourselves up for success. No matter how small the initial negotiation is, we should be looking to build our book of contacts and build relationships that we can call upon further down the line with new business opportunities.

When buying a car, a top integrative negotiator uses his persuasive skills to uncover information about the car salesperson, the car and the opportunity. This shows interest at this deeper level, moves the conversation to a more cooperative zone and allows mutual respect and understanding to build. It also creates a bridge between the buyer and seller upon which information can flow. The integrative negotiator exchanges information with the car salesperson. However, this does not mean that it would reveal all of their motivations, price points and needs right away. Warning: I want to be absolutely clear here, just so that I can be absolutely sure we aren't getting our wires crossed. Being an integrative negotiator does not mean we suddenly reveal everything, it means we are open to information exchange. There is a huge difference because if you reveal your complete motivations, budget and motivation you are likely to get taken advantage of through emotional leverage. Once a seller knows why you want the car, this motivation can be used emotionally as a benchmark to apply added pressure. The difference between this and an integrative negotiator is the mindset, but let's be clear here, you are still streetwise, even though you are open to working together.

The principles at play in this integrative style reveal more information, which in turn informs the negotiating pair where they need to focus their attention to make a successful deal. By aiming to understand the other side, the buyer has moved the negotiation into the trust building stage (which we will go into in greater detail later). This is a key stage for the negotiation to progress. The buyer and the seller would, in effect, work as a team to solve the problems identified (e.g. price, warranty, time frame, discount, quality, size) by challenging the assumptions around each factor. Each component would consist of a mini negotiation whereby prioritisation would determine what was agreed.

In essence, the integrative approach is dramatically more successful than any other method because both parties are overcoming the problems together. This is especially true in the case of repeat business that builds on previous dealings. Both parties have the opportunity to benefit from approaching negotiation from the integrative mindset – by sharing information, challenging assumptions and creating new pockets of value.

This is an important point that should be forever etched into your mind. Try not to think of negotiation as what's currently on the table, but an opportunity to expand the size of the pie.

Humans have been given the gift of higher-level thinking, the ability to look down on a situation and themselves, to get above it and apply both their logical and creative thought processes. This is where we win as negotiators. If we can design systems and processes with collaborative problem-solving principles at the core, then we can take the negotiation into a new sphere of possibility. Instead of just making transactions, we can transform situations and innovate.

And the good news is that's the way the world is going. There is an innovation race currently on; we are in an information economy. In the industrial revolution, it was those with the machines that had the wealth, now it's those with information.

If you think about it, nature has always been this way. If we take something on face value without recognising and searching for the possibility in a curious and explorative way, then we will touch only the surface of the potential. Think of an acorn, on the surface it looks like a regular nut. There's nothing noteworthy, but over time and given the right elements and environment, it will transform into something huge and beautiful. If we just looked at the unspectacular acorn and wrote it off, then we would never have grown a powerful oak.

Each negotiation is like an acorn. Whether it transforms into a tree that gives life to other trees and produces a healthy forest depends solely on recognising the potential and consistently maintaining the right environment for it to flourish. It starts with your mindset. Treat each negotiation like an acorn that you can choose to nurture and grow. In any integrative negotiation, we are nurturing that acorn together because we both understand that the overall value, created by working collaboratively to give it what it needs, is greater than the sum of our parts.

Issues, positions and interests

> "The very best negotiators take a broader approach to setting up and solving the right problem. With a keen sense of the potential value to be created as their guiding beacon, these negotiators are game-changing entrepreneurs. They envision the most promising architecture and take action to bring it into being."
>
> James K Sebenius, Vice Chair of Practice-Focused Research, PON Executive Committee, Harvard Business School

Now there's a quote to whet your appetite. The team that created the 7 elements I have covered in the **frameworks** section earlier in this chapter is best known for its development of the theory of 'principled negotiation'. This is a concept that focused on the interests of parties rather than their positions. It is centred around building opportunities for mutual gain. For more information on the topic, I recommend reading *Getting To YES: Negotiating Agreement Without Giving In* by Roger Fisher, Bill Ury and Bruce Patton. First published in 1981, the concepts presented in this book still hold true today. But back to James K Sebenius; he states that there are three components to any negotiation. These are:

1. Issues - the things that are being negotiated
2. Positions - your 'stance' on the issues
3. Interests - what's affected by reaching an agreement

For example, the **issue** in a negotiation might be the price. The **position** could then be: 'I want the price to be as high as possible while reaching an agreement.' The subsequent **interest** may be the commission that I receive for making a sale.

You can start to see that the negotiation can already be quite complex to begin with, depending on the importance weighting that is attributed to each of these three variables on either side of the bargaining table, and that's even before emotions, time pressures and poor communication enter the arena.

Phases of the negotiation process and how I do things differently

Now let's think about the process of negotiation. Negotiation theory states that there are three phases.

3 Phases of the negotiation process

Exchange of Information | Bargaining | Closing

Well, first off, let me tell you that this 3-step system fails to mention the most important step of the negotiation process: the preparation stage. We will cover this in more detail in Chapter 2, but preparation is key for any successful negotiator.

4 Phases of the negotiation process

| Negotiation Preparation | Exchange of Information | Bargaining | Closing |

Each phase of negotiation requires different behaviours.

In the **negotiation preparation** stage, it's imperative that we focus on what we want out of the negotiation itself. We must have absolute clarity about this before we move any further into the process. Proceeding without this information could undermine the negotiations, our reputation and our confidence, because we are more likely to stumble, take wrong turns and, ultimately, get taken advantage of when we don't know what it is we want. Therefore, we must exhibit a thoughtful and contemplative approach to negotiation preparation. This is your time for the due diligence and self-examination that later enables us to hit a home run.

In the **exchange of information** phase, we must behave in a way that engenders trust, such as collaborative discussion, explanation and active listening. The purpose of this stage is to uncover more details regarding the purpose of the agreement and establish the boundaries (upper and lower limits) of the deal. It is also a fundamental step in the formation of trust building. By sharing information about ourself, such as our interests, family and friends, we are opening up and bridging the gap between us. As we firmly establish key details that surround the proposed deal, like the time frame, price, needs and volume, we begin to move into the bargaining phase of the process. This can happen during one conversation or it could be over the course of a number of meetings. It will depend on the context and the scope of the deal that is in discussion.

In the **bargaining stage** of negotiation, we should seek to understand through active listening, empathy and emotional intelligence. It's at this stage that a series of mini-negotiations will take place surrounding the specifics of the deal. When we break the deal down into its specific components, we will need to agree on elements in isolation, while still taking into consideration the bigger picture. This is why it's so important to get into the specifics during the preparation phase, as this will help you to sequence the issues in order of priority. That way you will know what's worth fighting for and what you can leave.

The process of negotiation may take many twists and turns before reaching the closing phase. It may also reach the closing phase and then return to the exchange of information phase, as new details and contexts emerge.

The **closing phase** is where you should push for a commitment, e.g. 'So what price can you do?' or 'Have you seen something today that would suit your needs?'

The key here is to move the negotiation into deal territory. We are talking about hard facts and figures here. In closing, I find that hand gestures and eye contact increase. It's important that the other side know that you are requesting an answer and you intend to be heard. They need to feel from your body language that you mean business and the negotiation is now in the agreement stage.

It's like shifting gears in a car, it can be done ever so smoothly or clunkily with a big jolt that everyone is aware of. What is said at this stage matters, you are driving for action, results and commitment. In my opinion, this stage is incredibly easy to mess up because it takes guts to put an offer out there and risk being rejected. It is also easy to think you have closed when in your heart of hearts, you know you've only loosely closed the deal, and if push came to shove there is no actual commitment.

I find it helpful to use a time-bound trigger to close as it places a sense of urgency on the deal. Get to the point, and rather than ask if they want to do the deal, tell them: 'How much can I put you down for.' Plant that seed of commitment and start nudging them towards a close. The speed and tone of our voice can change in the closing phase. Watch out for this and you'll notice that people tend to speak quicker and have a high intonation when pushing for agreement. One strategy that people looking to close use is to create a sense of momentum by speaking more rapidly, skipping over important details and increasing the intensity of the conversation. This acts as a mechanism for forcing a decision because the other side is bombarded and feels obliged to accept the deal to end this cycle, without knowing what they have fully agreed to. In this strategy, the other side feels they have no choice but to agree. I mention this, not as a strategy for admiration, but rather as one to watch out for, so that you know when you are the victim of someone pushing for a close through force, rather than mutual exchange.

My number one tip for closing is, always follow up what was verbally agreed in writing and ask for an email confirmation back that the party agrees. If they don't respond then you should take this as a massive red flag that the deal has not been closed.

When closing verbally, repeat back what has been said so that you both can be sure that you have understood the terms correctly. Then follow up on email. Pursue this stage with all that you have got, as this is not the time to drop the ball and start celebrating the win. This is where a high level of concentration, discipline and best practise are required so that you are persistent in your follow-up requests to get an agreement in writing and you are not swayed by the other party's persuasion. I should warn you that you will get objections, including statements such as: 'But we are friends, don't you trust me, the deal is done' or 'Yeah, yeah fine, I'll shoot over confirmation tomorrow,' and then nothing comes... This is where you will need to take your A-game and have a disciplined approach. Think about it, this form of written confirmation actually protects you both, will save your future relationship from misunderstanding and deviousness. If the other side is not willing to put pen to paper and commit, then I urge you to think about the costs of accepting the deal without confirmation.

The reality is, you can execute your planning perfectly, hit the information exchange eloquently and bargain with the tenacity and grace of a chess grandmaster, but if you leave this closing phase undone, you'll find that your negotiations unravel quicker than a toddler with a ball of string. To close, you will need to be bold, clear and leave no stone unturned. If you have a question the back of your mind, ask it now. This is not the time to assume you have all the detail, this is the time for clarity. In closing, you can afford to be direct because you value the relationship that is being built and, therefore, you don't want any future misunderstandings in the business relationship to occur. If the other side questions you on why you are pushing for answers, commitments and hard facts and figures, you can explain this to them. By being thorough, you are ultimately protecting the future of the relationship. If the deal is going to fall down, it is most at risk at this stage. But this is also when the best deals are formulated and stitched together seamlessly. If the other side looks shifty, uncomfortable or is wavering in their commitment, this is a red flag and should be probed immediately. Call it out or it will come back to bite you later on.

Negotiations are also subject to the ebbs and flows of life's rich tapestry. The goal of any successful negotiation – and this is where the 'Art' comes in – is to be able to streamline the negotiation while building a valued relationship that allows for truly innovative solutions to be unlocked.

1.4 Things to Remember in Any Negotiation:

Butterflies before doing the deal

Remember this: there's no harm in asking and don't make it bigger than it needs to be. There will be more deals, this is just one of them. Learn from it, have fun with it and don't sweat it. 'Either I win or I learn.' So what if they get angry or don't like your terms? Keep your cool. Proceed and explain why what you've presented has merit. Not all deals will go smoothly; that's just the nature of it when you're dealing with multiple people with different personalities. The best thing you can do is figure out those people you like to do business with and those you don't. Reading and understanding people is a key skill. It will help you to understand where you want to do business. Some people just don't work together; they rub each other up the wrong way and trust is limited. This is always going to be a bad situation so just walk away from it and find someone new.

Gut instinct

My advice in everything is to follow your gut; you will know deep down whether it seems like an opportunity for you to get stuck into. If in doubt, follow your gut. This also applies if you are ripping someone off; you will know when you have got too good a deal. It won't feel good. Listen to your gut; find a deal that makes sense. Often, when I do a deal that's too good, I end up breaking the deal down for the other person and moving the needle back in their favour because my focus is on the relationship. I want to go into business with those I trust and, ultimately, people want the same. If it comes out later down the line that you screwed them, it's not great for the long-term prospects of the relationship or your reputation, for that matter. You can have a reputation as a ruthless negotiator. A shark. A taker. A hustler. But if no one wants to do business with you, what's the good in that? My philosophy is to focus on the win-win and, as I state throughout this book, the sweetest deals are the ones where you both profit in some way.

The other part to all of this is you will sometimes get taken for a ride; you'll get burnt, a good deal will turn out to be a not so good deal, and you will get taken in by the smooth-talking sales person. This is all part of it. Don't for one second beat yourself up over it; learn from it and see that this is all par for the course.

It's like testing a start-up; you need to put some money through it to find out where the problems and issues are. This is only lost capital if you don't fix the issues and listen to feedback. The same applies to negotiation. When I complete a deal that's less favourable than I initially thought, I go back to the drawing board and write it down. I then work out what led to me to think it was a good deal, and what I learn from it. Over time, your gut instinct will tell you that you've been here before; you'll start to have moments of déjà vu more frequently and recognise intuitively when it just doesn't feel right.

Deal in deadlock

When a deal has reached deadlock and got 'stuck' on a few points that either side deems to be non-negotiable, we must look for specific differences between each of the requests. James Sebenius says that 'differences help drive deals'. By focusing our attention on where the differences in motivation, needs and requests lie, we give the deal a new life. As the old saying goes, 'what we focus on expands'. Therefore, by directing our attention to the differences and moving away from the deadlock, we allow areas of agreement to be found; thus, expanding and creating the positive momentum that can be harnessed to bring the deal back to life.

Quick Summary

- Negotiation frameworks provide an overview of the topics that we must truly master to become top negotiators
- There are two types of negotiations according to theory – integrative and distributive
- There are four key stages to any negotiation: preparation, exchange of information, bargaining and closing

Activity

Are you aware of all the negotiations that are taking place around you? Take time out to notice how much negotiation is going on around you. Two hours should be sufficient. Starting tomorrow, note down where you see negotiations taking place and which style you see happening (either integrative or distributive). This could be at work or walking around town. The goal here is to build your negotiation awareness and also to make you pay attention to the amount of negotiations you experience directly or indirectly. This will help you to identify opportunities and uncover your own negotiation preferences.

2

STAMINA

'What are your choices when someone puts
a gun to your head?'

Harvey Spector,
high-flying lawyer in TV
legal drama, *Suits*.

IN THIS CHAPTER, I will show you a number of individuals who have achieved their audacious goals, overcome great adversity and gone to extraordinary lengths to see their vision come to life. I'll then delve into what we can learn from these highly valuable and inspiring game changers.

This chapter should be read and re-read whenever you face a challenging negotiation. The purpose is to push you harder and ensure that you know that it is, indeed, possible. It is the creativity and the character that you apply to the situation, when all the doors stay closed, which will ensure you overcome it. Stamina in negotiations is important, as there will be times when it will be hard to see the light at the end of the tunnel and you will want to throw in the towel. But knowing this, you are stronger than you actually feel in that moment, and you will find a way to keep going. After all, it is not the mistakes we make that define our success, it's how rigorously and consistently we apply the lessons that they teach us. To round off the chapter, I'll give you some strategies for improving your mental toughness and fortitude.

2.1 Know Your Choices

First cab off the rank, negotiation is about stamina. Ask yourself this question: do you have the will power to put something back together again or seek out other avenues and options when all roads point towards a dead end?

Over the seasons of *Suits*, Harvey imparts much advice to his young enthusiastic protégé, Mike, as he begins down the road to becoming a fully-fledged lawyer. One conversation that is particularly relevant to negotiation is when Harvey teaches Mike about broadening his mind. It goes like this:

Harvey: What are your choices when someone puts a gun to your head?

Mike: What are you talking about? You do what they say or they shoot you.

Harvey: WRONG. You take the gun, or you pull out a bigger one. Or you call their bluff. Or you do any one of 146 other things. If you can't think for yourself, then maybe you're not cut out for this.

And Harvey's got it right; we need to think about our choices. It may not always be black and white when we're negotiating and there are any number of ways that we can get to the result we want. The question is, in the heat of the moment, do we think of them?

This is where training comes into play, and being able to control our emotions. Break down the problems into small chunks and apply blue-sky thinking to them.

The difference between an average negotiator and a world-class one is the ability to roll with the punches and still come out on top. A world-class negotiator understands that she must leverage her mind to stay in the game; there is *always* another option. She recognises that by keeping her wits about her, she will overcome whatever obstacles are sent her way by sheer mental agility and perseverance. When it comes to stamina, world-class negotiators stay the course. They have a goal in mind and are able to use ideation techniques to think outside the box for innovative solutions.

To take this example further. The next time you are in a jam and something doesn't go the way you expected it to, remember this conversation between Harvey and Mike and spend a moment thinking about what you *haven't* thought of yet that could help.

Question: do you have what it takes to rebuild, regroup and carry on?

The path to successful negotiation isn't always easy, and is rarely a straight line. It takes struggle and fight no matter what level you are at. A world-class negotiator keeps an open mind and is always eager to learn from others, to hear a new perspective and take on a new challenge.

If you've ever watched a world series poker game you'll know how quickly the stakes can turn. Negotiation is like that; the struggle isn't over until you say it is and if you run out of chips you need to come up with another way to progress.

2.2 Stamina

Stamina is about having grit when the chips are down and the doors are staying closed. It's about refocusing your energies and working smarter and harder to produce the results. In the toughest negotiations, when our minds and our bodies are pushed to their limits, it's important to remember to keep the basics down pat; remember to eat, drink and keep your priorities straight. Like setting out on a long adventure, stamina combined with absolute willpower is what gets us to the end, but if we fail to look after ourselves we only serve to hinder our progress.

We know that life isn't always a straight line but negotiation requires us to push further than that. It challenges us to understand that the rules of today might not apply tomorrow and that what's possible is dictated by our determination to stay the course and develop alternative ways to create opportunities for ourselves.

It's not about waiting; it's about getting to grips with your own creativity and finding that voice within us that says, 'I will carry on', even when you feel like all the roads are blocked. That's your fight and that's what you must engage with, even if there only seems to be a slim chance of success. Remember, if it is possible, it can happen, and if it can happen, you need to figure out the steps to make that a reality. It can be closer than we think; we just need to have stamina.

2.3 STAMINA CASE STUDY

There are some excellent examples of people from different parts of the world, in different industries and situations who didn't give up in this world; history shows us this repeatedly.

Jack Ma

Think of Jack Ma, Founder and Executive Chairman of the Alibaba Group, one of the world's largest e-commerce businesses. He has taken the title of China's richest man, and his story is one of humility, perseverance and a burning desire to keep on going.

Jack was born in 1964 in Hangzhou, Zhejiang Province, China, a picturesque place about two hours from Shanghai that is well known for its natural beauty. It's also known for its tea production, fine silk and manufacturing. Marco Polo once stopped by for a visit and is reported to have called it 'beyond dispute the finest and the noblest in the world'.

Jack learned to speak English here from an early age. To speed up his progress, he would ride his bike each day more than 70 minutes in each direction to go and speak to English speaking guests who were staying at Hangzhou International Hotel. Talk about dedication to the cause!

Jack had a rough time at school and was bullied, though he was never scared of those who were bigger than him. He also struggled to get into college. The entrance exam was held once a year, and it took him four years and four painful attempts to secure a place.

Early on in his career, Jack applied for over 30 different jobs and was rejected by all of them. Famous quotes from Jack include, 'I even went to KFC when it came to my city. Twenty-four people went for the job. Twenty-three were accepted. I was the only guy…' Jack also had an interview for a job with the police, but they said: 'You're no good,' and he applied to Harvard University 10 times and got rejected 10 times.

In the 1980s, Jack graduated with a BA in English, met his wife and began teaching at a local school, but it wasn't until 1995 that on a visit to America, he found his calling in the world of online business. After two failed online ventures, Jack founded Alibaba in 1999, an online marketplace connecting manufacturers and their products to direct customers, cutting out the middleman. His vision was so strong that he convinced 17 of his friends to join him and invest in the business.

Things really started to look up in October 1999 when Alibaba raised $5m from Goldman Sachs and an another $20m from Softbank in funding. The Alibaba dream was on and very much beginning to take shape.

Fast-forward a few more years to 2005 and Yahoo! came knocking with an offer of $1 billion dollars in investment for a 40% stake in the business. (This turned out to be a very wise move; when Alibaba listed on the New York Stock Exchange in 2014, it broke the record for the largest initial public offering in the world by raising $25 billion, and Yahoo! made a cool $10 billion. That's a 900% ROI.)

It's important not to forget that Jack's philosophy of having fun can be found through all of the twists and turns, the mishaps, and the changes in direction. For example, when Alibaba first became profitable, Jack went out and bought the whole team silly string to go wild with. It's also well documented that Jack encourages his employees to do handstands to keep their energy levels up. This mix of fun and business is parallel to another famous mogul, Sir Richard Branson. It's safe to say that business and fun go together just like negotiation and fun do. When you are out to solve problems, influence high stakes deals and put it all on the line, a little fun can often be the secret ingredient that makes all the difference.

So, as we've seen, Jack was rejected from a number of jobs, from KFC right through to the police department and Harvard University. He failed at two start-up ventures and yet still went on to hold the title of China's richest person with a net worth of US$ 37.4 billion (August 2017). This is evidence that stamina is important in both getting the deal and negotiation. Jack is quoted as telling the Alibaba team of employees when they started out: 'We will make it because we are young and we never, never give up.'

It seems easy when we look back at a rags-to-riches story like this to think 'well that was them, and this is me,' but what this type of thinking misses are the hours of perseverance, the courage it takes to get up and rebuild after failure, and to learn from mistakes and come back stronger.

The problem is we are inundated with stories of those who've made it; and the media makes it look so damn easy. They often explain what they did, but miss out the sheer magnitude of the struggle, the late nights, the forgotten weekends, as well as the 18-hour days, the anxiety, the blood, sweat and tears and the graft that changes your stars.

The thing is, we could all be only a few steps or chance meetings away from our $37 billion fortune, it can just take a few moments of inspiration. The question is, what makes us so interested, engaged and motivated that we will keep on going for it, whatever it takes? There's no point having stamina if we don't know why we are doing it. The purpose is what drives the impact, and therefore understanding why you are negotiating is a crucial driver of motivation that will keep your stamina tank full.

Adam Grant (of whom I am a big fan and will reference a lot during this journey), Organisational Psychologist, Wharton Professor and *New York Times* bestselling author of *Give and*

Take, *Originals* and *Option B,* with Sheryl Sandberg, COO of Facebook, tells us the story of a Giver who struggled to stand up for himself in negotiations. He wasn't able to execute a fair deal in the salary negotiation of a new job until he realised that it wasn't just him he was negotiating for. He realised that it wasn't just him he was fighting for; it was his wife and his newborn child as well. This change in perspective caused a change in him. His motivation to push for a better deal by explaining his situation to his new employer gained him over $70,000 in financial rewards. By engaging with his purpose, he increased his stamina, and this new-found way of thinking allowed him to push past his feelings of discomfort and negotiate on behalf of his family.

The truth is, becoming a skilful negotiator is all well and good, but knowing why we are doing it is where the fun can be found and is what builds stamina. That is why keeping our values intact during negotiation is so important.

When Alibaba IPO'd on the New York Stock Exchange, Jack told his staff he hoped they would use their wealth to 'become a batch of genuinely noble people who are able to help others, be kind and be happy'. How cool is that! What a legend that guy is. He is true to his values, understands the value that Alibaba is bringing to the world, and because of this, had the stamina to keep on going when all roads pointed to 'no'.

When you've identified that 'something' that's worth it, you won't stop until the job is done; that's where negotiation can help and it's the kind of attitude you need to have when your facing monumental challenges.

Being able to influence, having the agility to see new possibilities where others see none; that's what will set you apart from the rest and allow you to grow stronger as a result.

As you learn to trust your instinct more frequently, you will naturally become more resilient. As you push harder and develop new methods of creating opportunities and opening more doors, you will grow.

The more you practice, the more you flourish. It might even seem that you're not growing, learning or managing to open any doors at all, but you'll be surprised. Even the tougher conversations will sharpen your senses and heighten your understanding, so that you can try a different approach next time.

Jack Ma Lessons:

1. **Go the extra mile** – life is a journey and we must do whatever we can to inch our way forwards to achieve our vision by using whatever we can to improve.
2. **Smile when you're winning, smile when you're learning** – Jack's life story is a tale of repeated rejection, continued persistence and acting on opportunity.
3. **Be humble** – even on the day his company went stratospheric, setting world records on the stock exchange and making a number of employees millionaires overnight, Jack reminds us that being humble is the way to act in every situation.

2.4 Mindset and Mental Toughness

This is important because it's always tougher than expected, and will take greater persistence, courage and mental fortitude than we have allowed for. The good news is there's plenty that you can do to increase your mental toughness and fine-tune your mindset for success in negotiation.

When Richard Branson wanted to impress a girl, he phoned up an estate agent and enquired about buying an island in the Caribbean. Using his charm, he managed to convince them to fly him out on an all-expenses paid trip to go and see the island, under one condition, he was allowed to bring a guest. Talk about a first date! Just kidding, it was the second. That island was Necker Island in the British Virgin Islands, and it had a price tag of $6 million.

Richard liked the island so much that he decided to make an offer. With the price tag being so hefty, Richard offered the most he could afford at the time, which was $100,000.

So, let's break this down. Here you have a young Richard Branson out on a mission to woo his girl, positioning himself as 'in the market' for an island in the Caribbean, and offering 98.34% less than the asking price. To cut a long story short, the offer was rejected and Richard and his girl (who was his future wife) were sent packing.

A year or so later, Richard got a call from the estate agent. The owner of the island had fallen on tough times and needed to make a quick sale. Although they couldn't match Richard's initial bid, they were open to negotiation. Quick-witted Richard upped his initial offer by 80% to $180,000 and it was accepted. That's still a 97% discount from the original price of the Caribbean island ($180k/$6m)! Richard had visions of using the island as a haven away from the distractions of modern day life, that rock stars could use as a luxury retreat to fly out to and record their music for his company Virgin Records.

The point of this tale is, we don't know what's possible until we ask, and if Richard Branson was pulling off stunts like this in 1978, then it's proof that we can all think bigger than we currently do.

If you haven't read it, Sir Richard Branson's autobiography, *Losing My Virginity*, is a phenomenal example of how mindset and mental toughness play a role in getting you to the top of your field. The book follows the story of Richard through the ages and explains how he built his empire, and more importantly, details the struggles, obstacles and near misses he overcame to achieve it. This book is a mandatory read for any potential world-class negotiator because the tenacity and level of self-determination exhibited is an excellent example of how to make things possible against all odds.

Mindset and mental toughness in negotiation is key. Possession of this element is like oxygen to humans. Without it we don't work, and neither will successful negotiation.

Visualisation

The first step is visualisation. Jim Carrey, the guy who brought us hugely successful 90s movies, like *Ace Ventura*, *The Mask* and *Dumb and Dumber*, used this technique for years before he was famous. He reportedly wrote himself a cheque for $10 million dollars for 'acting services rendered' that, when stuffed into his wallet, acted as a daily reminder that he would make it.

In doing this, Jim was telling himself and signalling to the universe that he could and would go the distance. Then, low and behold, a few years later, guess what? He got a big payday for the movie *Dumb and Dumber that was* $10 million dollars.

Visualising the future and the outcome that you want is important if you want the universe to move in a certain direction or manifest a certain outcome. Visualising it actually happening is the first step to making it happen. By visualising success in the negotiation, including how it will feel, what you will say and running through the actions you will take, you are priming the mind so that it will feel more familiar when you take on the negotiation.

Self-talk

Self-talk is super important, and more specifically negative self-talk, i.e. what you tell yourself, day in and day out. You must believe with 100% certainty that it *can* happen, for it *to* happen. This is because your beliefs drive your actions, as we've already discussed, and the amount of potential you think something has of coming off.

Listen to the conversation and the story that you tell yourself on a daily basis. When you see an opportunity, what does your mind immediately jump to? 'That can't happen' or 'that's impossible'?

Are you telling yourself a story which is based on beliefs that no longer serve you? If so, it's time to drop those beliefs and focus on ones that support your goals, dreams and vision.

Finding your why

Humans are emotional creatures and so it stands to reason that emotional motivators play a large part in how successful we will be at something. In the book *177 Mental Toughness Secrets of the World Class,* Steve Siebold states the number one reason top coaches question their athletes when they start coaching them is to 'tap into a stream of gold'. When athletes start answering in terms of *why* they feel the way they do, instead of *what* they feel, the coaches know they are onto something. This allows the athletes to connect their practice to their purpose and enables them to achieve high levels of performance when required.

Figuring out what drives us, what gets us out of bed in the morning and pumped is a key part of the equation. When we know why we are doing something, we can train ourselves to tap into that motivational stream when things get tough.

This centres us and brings us back in line with our vision and the bigger picture. When we get stressed and anxiety and pressure mount, our world gets narrower and the range of options that seems available to us closes, and the world becomes a dark and gloomy place.

One way to open it up and gain some much-needed perspective is to refocus on our 'why'. Once we have that in our mind, obstacles, people and problems don't seem so big anymore and we can start to see solutions where there were none before.

Habits

Daily rituals boil down to one word: 'habit'. The world class have a number of resilience-building activities baked into their daily routine, ranging from meditation to getting a well-earned sleep, to broadening the mind through inspirational articles, books and speaking events. This is because it is paramount to have a routine that allows you to get off the dance floor and onto the balcony to see what's going on and spot the opportunities. This principle of taking time to get off the dance floor to observe what's going on from the balcony comes from Heifetz and Linsky's 2002 book, *Leadership on the Line*: *Staying alive through the dangers of leading*. The idea behind this principle is that your attention on the dance floor is focused mainly on your dance partner and making sure that you don't step on toes or crash into the other dancers. To get a real perspective on what is really going on the dance floor, i.e. to get a big picture of the business or situation, we must step off the dance floor and go up on to the balcony, as it is there that we can see how the others are dancing, what songs get the most dancers up out of their seats and where the dancers tend to congregate. Most of all it allows us to spot what's not happening and the areas of opportunity. If we want to effect change, then we must return to the dance floor and put our insights from the balcony into action. Of course, this is just a metaphor for how to gain a broader sense of the business and affect change. In our everyday lives, its paramount that we have rituals that allow us to routinely get some 'me time' away from the noise.

Exercise, audiobooks, journaling and travel all provide outlets that allow the mind to grow in resilience.

Beliefs

We've touched on these already; that's because they are fundamentally so important. Make sure that you learn to check in with yourself on a regular basis to address your beliefs; update the ones that are no longer serving you and drop any that are no longer relevant. This is important because holding on to the beliefs we have inherited from others, like our parents, siblings or friends, can cause us to act in ways that are incongruent to our actual values. This causes what psychologists call cognitive dissonance, a type of psychological stress that occurs when we behave in a way that is not in line with our beliefs. By regularly reviewing our beliefs, to make sure that they are in fact our own beliefs and updating or editing them where necessary, we are free to take actions that carry us forward and align with our vision of the world. This mainly stems from the fact that we adopt the beliefs and values of those closest to us when we are growing up. Then, as we get older, we grow up and create our own belief system. Naturally, just like a computer, problems arise when we fail to update it.

2.5 Bold Beliefs Case Study

Elon Musk

I just want to spend a little time introducing you to the one and only Elon Reeve Musk. If you haven't heard of him already, he's a South African-born Canadian-American entrepreneurial guru/inventor/investor/engineer.

He is worth a cool $17.4 billion and is the founder and CEO of SpaceX, a company whose core mission is to revolutionise space technology with the ultimate goal of enabling people to live on other planets (it might seem like science fiction, but this is taken direct from spacex.com).

If that wasn't a big enough goal, he is also the CEO of Tesla, a company that specialises in electric cars, lithium-ion battery energy storage and solar panels (through the acquisition of Solar City). Tesla has already surpassed the 200,000-unit mark in global sales (March 2017) and is gaining traction in the much sort after Chinese market.

To give you an idea of who Elon Musk is, let's start by exploring his current goals.

Musk's Goals:

- To reduce the cost of human spaceflight by a factor of 10
- To send humans to Mars within 10–20 years (stated in a 2011 interview)
- To establish a Mars colony by 2040, with a population of 80,000 (Source: Ashlee Vance's biography on Musk).

Now let's look at what Musk currently has in action:

Musk publicly stated that Space X aims to start production of its BFR (Big F@*kin Rocket) spacecraft in Q2 of 2018, when he spoke at the International Astronautical Congress in Adelaide, 29 September 2017. This is for the intended purpose of launching two rockets as early as 2022 to go as a cargo supply mission to Mars, where it will drop off mining, power and life-support resources. Following this, he revealed that they hope to launch two crewed ships and two cargo ships to go to Mars by 2024 and begin to set up a colony by building a base for future trips.

Musk is a guy who has never been afraid to put it all on the line and go after what he wants. He built an internet start-up from the ground up in the 90s called Zip2 (think Google Maps plus Yellow Pages), sold it for $307m and then reinvested his share of the profits ($22m) into X.com, an online bank he set up in 1999.

X.com later became PayPal when it merged with Confinity (a similar start-up founded by Peter Theil). He repeated this risk-taking investment strategy, and what was considered by some as insanity, a few years later when he invested all of his $180m earnings (from the sale of PayPal to eBay for $1.5 billion) into three separate ventures over four years. These were Space X ($100m, 2002), Tesla ($70m, 2004) and Solar City ($10m, 2006). Here is an example of a multimillionaire backing himself to win and making his dreams a reality.

Even before the sale of PayPal had been completed, Elon got to work. He began consuming all he could on the subject of space rockets. Musk's certainty that he can reduce the cost of human spaceflight by creating reusable launch vehicles and rockets is admirable, and we should take note of his self-belief and ability to proceed even when the goals we are hunting are bigger than most.

Fast forward a few years and now comes the stamina that is required. 2008 happened, the global financial crisis was in full swing and the auto industry was hit harder than most. Not the time to try to launch a new car, let alone one in a practically untouched sector. It's safe to say that the automobile industry tanked; the capital dried up and Tesla was hemorrhaging cash left right and centre. Tesla had failed to deliver on its product timelines and had yet to get a single product to market. Silicon Valley was watching with bated breath and critics were eating them for breakfast.

Musk scraped together all that he had left and invested his last $20m to keep Tesla afloat. He gave personal guarantees to customers waiting for an order, and to refund in full in the event of the business collapsing. At the same time, Musk was also in the middle of a divorce from his wife.

Along the road, SpaceX wasn't having any luck either. It was down to its final rocket, with the last three attempts ending in explosions somewhere over the Pacific. The fourth and final launch had to work because there was simply no money left in the kitty. Musk was now funding both of these companies on his own coin, driven by the fundamental understanding that he had built solid companies, and that all they needed was time. He was breathing life into these companies, giving them the time they needed to prove their greatness to the world.

On 28 September 2008, the winds of change were upon the Space X camp and Falcon 1 became the first ever privately developed liquid-propelled carrier rocket to successfully reach low Earth orbit, a world's first in the history of space exploration. NASA was so impressed it handed Musk a

$1.5 billion contract for the commercial resupply service programme for 12 flights of the Falcon 9 to the International Space Station.

Breaking records seems to be something of a tradition at SpaceX. In 2016, it made history again by landing a Falcon 9 on a drone ship at sea, taking the possibility of a reusable spacecraft one step further.

Interestingly, like Apple's Founder Steve Jobs, Musk also opts for the $1 per year salary, and chooses to be rewarded by performance-based bonuses instead. It's clear that this guy backs himself to go after big goals and then wills them into existence. This is another form of putting it all on the line, and putting his stamina to work by leaving himself no other option but to succeed.

So what can we learn from Musk's approach? Here we have a guy who is relentless in the pursuit of his mission. He states his goal, however outlandish, inconceivable or unfathomable it may seem, and then outlines steps to go after it.

Lessons from Elon Musk:

1. **Belief** – Musk backs himself to win; he has absolute certainty that it will happen.
2. **Research** – When Musk decides to do something, he researches the topic feverishly, inside and out, so that he can have an informed conversation with any manner of specialists.
3. **Forward thinking** – Musk thinks ahead, way ahead, just look at his goals. He wants to solve the world's biggest problems on a global scale. Therefore, he is open-minded and thinks beyond the obvious by predicting the future, and then goes about creating it.

4. **Go big or go home** – He takes steps to create what Grant Cardone calls 'Massive Action' in *Sell or be Sold*. This is the level of action we need to win in the market. For example, Musk dropped out of his PhD at Stanford after two days because he 'couldn't stand to watch the internet go by,' he just had to get involved and make it better.

5. **Does whatever it takes** – There's no doubting that Musk has stamina. When he was creating Zip2, he and his brother slept at the office, showered at the local YMCA and worked night and day, coding to put Zip2 together.

Bias towards action

Taking action in a world of procrastination is the single biggest thing that you can do to increase your negotiating ability. So many people could be world class at negotiating if they dedicated a small portion of time each day to taking action. Making a commitment to practice and experiment, to step out of our comfort zone and give it a go is by far the quickest way to go from average to world class.

After all, 'we miss 100% of the chances we don't take'. This philosophy extends to negotiation; if you spot an opportunity to negotiate and you feel the urge inside you, or that little voice inside your head says 'go for it, just ask the question,' then please listen to it and make the request.

Victimisation, justification and blame

Here are three words that don't feature in the world-class negotiators' repertoire. World-class negotiators accept that they are completely responsible for how they show up during the negotiation and are also responsible for its success. If value is left on the table, they get distracted or the other party is simply better prepared, then they accept responsibility for the outcome, rather than look for excuses. If you want more success in your life, eradicate these destructive ways of thinking now.

Emotional criticism

Winston Churchill famously said, 'You'll never reach your destination if you stop to throw stones at every dog that barks' and the same line of thinking applies to world-class negotiators. They expect to be criticised because they are at the top of their game. It is all par for the course. Average performers are shocked when they get criticised by others and become emotionally caught up. The trick is not to get caught up in it.

Don't sweat it

Everyone gets chocked up and has a few big crashes every once in a while. The successful ones are those that can take lessons from failure and turn it into value. Mistakes tend to get a negative wrap in the corporate world. If you get the opportunity to negotiate in your job and it doesn't go the way you had planned, it can be a blow to your ego and you may fear that colleagues, and even your boss, may see you differently because of it. What companies need to realise is that they become way more valuable through making mistakes and learning from them. Rather than holding the mistake against you, or using it to keep you from ever negotiating again, they should be pushing you back into the ring to go again, as you have just came one step closer to becoming a negotiation expert.

We all get overwhelmed at times, especially when we want to make a good impression or prove our worth. One tip that I have found useful is not to think about the size of the deal or what it means to you until it's over. The best way I have found to operate is to keep the mind as clear as possible, focused only on the task at hand. This way I can engage my creative right side of my brain without forcing it, and come up with solutions, possibilities and options whilst staying logical, considered and rational minded through left-brain activities.

With practice, you'll be able to minimise the attention you place on the consequences of a negotiation and you'll suddenly realise: what's the big deal. When we feel like we are being judged on our ability to negotiate or extract the most value, for me anyway, this is when we start to clam up. I've been there, where you are, wanting to prove myself; not understanding that in order to be my best self, I need to let go of trying to prove it and focus only on the steps of best practice negotiation.

It was in my first job, when I was negotiating multiple deals throughout the day, that I actually felt most at ease because I had repeated exposure to negotiations. By building up a resilience, I was able to detach from the outcome and move on to the next one in a way that enabled me to negotiate uninhibited. It is this level of liberation that I want you all to reach. This is where you can pick up the phone or walk into any room and negotiate in a state of flow. You can anticipate the moves the other side will make because you have a clear head and will easily see the bigger picture and areas of opportunity for collaboration. Then, as if by magic, you will be able to pluck them from your consciousness and drop them, perfectly timed, into the conversation like you are the conductor of a symphony.

This may sound farfetched, but I am speaking from the heart and the mind when I explain this level of thinking. Negotiation changes from a practice and into an art form. You become the negotiation and are so in tune with what's going on that any anticipation or feelings of being overwhelmed dissolve because they are never given an opportunity to breathe.

To reach this state, you will need repeated exposure to negotiation. Ideally, these should be negotiations you conduct yourself so that you are in the driver's seat. That way, you can learn through first-hand experience, which is the most powerful form of learning.

The next time you catch yourself saying that you are 'bad at negotiation', stop and remind yourself that all you need is repeated exposure to negotiation. The quickest way to excel is to put your hand up and put yourself in the driver's seat.

I want to share with you J K Rowling's story as the final piece in this chapter on stamina because it will show you that if you have a vision and are determined to succeed no matter what, then you can overcome any roadblocks that fall in your path.

2.6 Persistence Case Study

J K Rowling

J K Rowling is a shining example of how people can use their resilience and stamina in the pursuit of an idea. In her case, it was an idea for a book that changed her stars. The world-famous author who brought us Harry Potter found herself as a single mother, living in her sister's flat in Scotland on government welfare. The idea for Harry Potter first came to Rowling back in 1990 while she was delayed on a train for four hours from Manchester to London. She recalls the idea for the book about a young boy who was into wizardry came fully formed into her mind. Sadly, her mother died of multiple sclerosis a few months later after many years of suffering, and it is well known that Rowling channelled her own feelings of loss into the first Harry Potter book. Despite all this, she carried on and decided to up sticks and move to Portugal to become an English teacher after seeing an ad in the newspaper. Here, she fell in love, married and had a child. In 1993, the marriage ended in divorce and that was when she decided to move to Edinburgh to live with her sister. She had three chapters written and a burning desire that she would succeed.

The book was rejected no less than 12 times by numerous well-known publishers before being taken on by Bloomsbury for a mere $1,500 advance.

This is grit at its finest. Not only did she cope with the repeated rejection and learned to stand back up again, while all the time believing in her ultimate goal for Harry Potter and believing the story deserved to be heard, but things around her were strikingly tough, personally and financially.

In 2014, J K Rowling was reported to be worth over $1 billion, having sold more than 400 million copies of her books.

Now that's impressive. It's not only about the money either; it's also about the possibility and the size of the opportunity. If we just keep finding a way to continue and pushing forward, even when the chips are down, by using our negotiation skills to open doors, just think what might we be able to accomplish.

Stamina is a force that drives you forward when you need to dig deep – the fire in your belly that drags you out of bed when you don't want to get up; the motivation to do more and be more than others think is possible.

J K Rowling's Lessons:

1. **Persistence is key** – J K Rowling made it her mission to keep going even in the face of 12 rejections.
2. **Determination** – the road maybe filled with bumps, but if we are steadfast and determined, we will get to our destination one way or another.

Quick Summary

- Stamina allows us to continue the pursuit of our goals in the face of hardship
- It's obsession that drives you on to achieve excellence
- There is much to learn from others
- Our goals come from our values and gaining self-awareness helps us to find our why
- Our habits and beliefs define how we get there
- The best way to improve is to get out there and experience it

Activity

Watch: *Suits*, particularly Season 1, Episode 2. Read: *177 Mental Toughness Secrets of the World Class* by Steve Siebold.

PART 2

GET READY TO NEGOTIATE

3

KNOW WHAT YOU WANT AND THEN PUT YOURSELF IN THE OTHER PERSON'S SHOES

Attract what you expect.
Reflect what you desire.
Become what you respect.
And mirror what you admire.

IN THIS CHAPTER, I'm going to show you the importance of knowing exactly what you want before you begin any sort of negotiation. The information that we uncover answers one specific question – what am I trying to achieve from this negotiation? By getting clear on this, we can form an accurate picture of our reservation price (the price at which we walk away). We can also weigh up and assess the costs and benefits of what's being offered and we can start to seek out alternatives. As we know, those with better alternatives tend to do better in negotiation. Knowing what you want isn't just about you, you also need to know and think deeply about what the other side wants. By identifying both sets of motivations you can trade issues to formulate a good deal and provide solutions that make you both better off whilst meeting your needs.

3.1 Know Your Desired Outcome

Think of it like going on a blind date. If you know beforehand that you are looking for a man who's ready to start a family, who is interested in fine arts and enjoys long walks on the beach while listening to Miley Cyrus, you are much better placed to ask the right questions and make a decision on how you want to move forward. You will have a goal for the desired outcome. This doesn't mean, however, that you are completely fixated on this singular outcome. Those who are the best at negotiating go into any negotiation with an open mind, an understanding of what they want to achieve and remain flexible on how to get there.

Now let's start with the basics; in win-win negotiation philosophy, first you must know what you want. It sounds simple, doesn't it? But it is crucial to any deal that you know exactly what you are after. If you do not know where your boundaries are, what your non-negotiables are, and who you would prefer to deal with, you have no way of defining the playing field.

The best negotiators have done their research; they know the following:

- The appropriate price range
- What a phenomenal deal is
- What an acceptable deal is
- What's a rip-off
- Who's the best (supplier, quality, reputation)
- What to look out for (red herrings, red flags)
- Why they are negotiating
- What questions to ask
- How to listen
- How to ask

Start with the question,' Above all else, what is the main thing I want to achieve from this deal?' as this is the perfect place to begin. Make it a habit to sit down before going into any negotiation and really think, 'What do I truly want from this?' If it is price, then how much are you willing to pay? If it's free accessories, then which ones do you prefer? If it's a flexible working solution, then how many days will it take and when?

The key is to be specific, so that when you make your request you can confidently and clearly identify in one short sentence what it is you want. By knowing what you want rather than making it up on the spot and freestyling it, you will be less likely to walk away agreeing to something that...

a) You didn't want.
b) Will cost you more than you wanted.
c) Wasn't really what you were after.

A well thought out plan of what you want is key to securing a good deal. In the media industry, we refer to it as 'having your ducks in a row'. What this means is that you know all the relevant information that you can possibility know about a deal, product, person, service and where you want to take the negotiation to make a profitable outcome before you engage in the negotiation itself.

Having a specific outcome in mind gives you the criteria to work with and a roadmap to follow. Imagine the details to be your guide, helping you to define the upper and lower limits of your agreement. For example, if you are offered the choice between a similar role and a redundancy package, how will you know which one to take and how will you know if you have made the right decision? By having a clear understanding upfront of where you intend to go, what you will accept, what you won't accept and how this plays into the bigger picture of your life, the established criteria will give you benchmarks to negotiate against. Ray Dalio, founder of Bridgewater, one of the most successful hedge funds the world has ever seen ($160 billion in assets under management, 2017), which he started from his two-bedroom apartment, argues: 'If you can get to the truth, then you can start asking yourself, how do I know I am right? In his book *Principles: Life and Work* he explains that knowing you are right is not enough, it's knowing why you are right that matters. He was writing in relation to the markets and trading commodities, stocks and bonds, so I am extrapolating here by applying it to our context of negotiation. The point is, by fully understanding the rationale behind our wants and desires, and then exploring them in detail, we are more likely to present a robust case during the negotiation, and have a greater understanding of where our flexibilities lie and be connected to the root motivation.

Understanding what we want in our mind's eye helps us to get clarity over where we are going with negotiation and makes our decision making easier. I am reminded of a time when my analytical and reasoning skills were tested to the absolute maximum and the responsibly on me to perform had never been higher.

When I was 19 years old, I joined my mother on a ski/business trip to the snowy Alps of Verbier, Switzerland. This trip remains very close to my heart as it was the first and last one that we took together, as she died due to an aggressive form of cancer only 11 months later.

Verbier was my ideal ski resort. It had everything, but what I was most drawn to was the lively atmosphere and the après ski. Luxurious, sprawling log cabins lined the mountainside and you could ski directly out of the front door. I had never seen anything like it, it was like a postcard.

I had joined my mother on this physiotherapy ski trip, the purpose was to learn new techniques and ski, the best of both worlds. As I wasn't a qualified physio I was left to my own devices for most of the trip and caught up with crew at meal times.

I ventured out every evening into town to explore the nightlife and have fun as teenage guys do.

Waking up one morning, I went off and hit the slopes. I was snowboarding down this pristine run going off piste, venturing a little further each time. I went up this bank of snow and then circled back down onto the main track each time. I was on my third run of the day loving being out in the sunshine, with the blue skies and fresh alpine air, when I decided this time to go over the crest of the snow bank to explore. No sooner had I done this, I found myself flat on my back hurtling at a rate of knots down the side of the mountain. I had hit a sheet of ice. I tried in vain to regain an upright position, but it was no use because both legs were fully extended due to my snowboard still being attached and the steep gradient of the mountain. I put my gloves out on the snow to try and slow down but I was going too fast and the friction of the gloves on the sheet ice burnt holes in them.

As I picked up speed, sliding faster and faster, I tried to focus on facing forwards so that I could see where I was going.

As I looked up, I could see the blue sly coming towards me and realised I was heading towards the edge of a cliff. With no idea of how high the drop was or what lay before me, I had no time to think. I saw a rock poking up out of the snow on the edge of the cliff.

Instantly, I reached down and unclipped my bindings that were keeping me trapped into the snowboard and as the snowboard flew off the edge of the cliff, I swung around on to my belly and grabbed onto a rock with all of my strength as the board and my legs flew over the edge of the cliff.

As I looked down below and hung clinging on to this rock, I saw my snowboard fall what must have been 200 feet down onto rocks and then continue, effortlessly gliding down the mountainside.

I hung there for what seemed like a few minutes, but was probably only ten seconds and took my breath. I said out loud to myself, 'Tim, this is the time to think clearly.' My adrenaline was pumping and I knew whatever I did in the next few minutes would be crucial for the rest of my life. I paused and focused. 'Tim, do not mess this up,' I said out loud, giving myself the pep talk of my life. I hauled my weight up so I was more centralised on the rock and not dangling as much in midair, trying to figure out what to do. I couldn't go back up from where I had come as one foot on that ice would have me over the edge and on my way to certain death.

I took it very slowly, and calculating each move in advance, shifted my weight, found my balance and stood up on the edge of the cliff.

No one knew I was here and although it was midday, I knew how fast the weather conditions could change on the mountain. I realised that the only way out of this situation was to try and climb down the cliff. Over to my left, I saw a pile of huge boulders and rocks and I made the decision to try and get to them, in the hope that they would be a safer option than where I was currently. Step by careful step, I made my way across the front of the cliff top, inching my way to these big boulders at the side. Before each step, I made sure I had my footing before putting my full weight down, and inch by inch, step by step, I crossed the cliff face. One wrong foot and I'd be gone. Even if I survived the fall, the chances of someone finding me were incredibly slim. As I got to the boulders on the left-hand side and a wave of relief passed over me. I remembered I wasn't done yet, I was still in great danger and so the challenge of the descent began. By making my way over to the left side of the cliff face, I gained a new vantage point and I could see a possible way forward. It went down through a dark tunnel, however, and I wasn't sure if the boulders would fall and crush me or if I would be going deep and deeper into a cavern with no exit. It was a risk I had to take.

With each move downwards, I made sure I could go back if I wanted to, and was extremely conscious that I didn't want to be trapped inside a cave on the side of a cliff with no exit that I couldn't get out of, as there would be even less chance of someone seeing me. I'd have more chance of being spotted up on the cliff face if they sent out a helicopter looking for me.

I kept talking to myself, keeping my spirits up and my mind focused on the adventure and the fact that I wasn't dead yet. The goal was just make it down safely. Take as long as you need, think about each move and don't get trapped or stuck.

After two hours of climbing and manoeuvring my way down, being extra careful not to disturb any of the rocks, I saw light. A wave of relief came over me, as it was possible I was going to do it. Still not celebrating until I had fully made it down to the bottom, my mind fixed on the goal – stay safe, look around you and make sure you can go backwards if you need to. I kneeled down on my belly and crawled out of a small gap at the bottom of the cliff some two hours later. I was hit with bright, dazzling light of the snow all around me reflecting off the sunlight. As I looked back up the cliff, it was much higher than I'd thought, and I realised that if it hadn't been for my quick thinking, when I took off the board, it would have taken me with it. There was no jumping down this one, as this was a game over type situation.

I couldn't believe it. The sense of elation I felt and the joy of living to see another day was huge and I talked to myself to keep my mind focused. I felt proud of myself but it had also taught me a big lesson, that mindset and focus is key. When you need to think clearly and it's just you and the world, you can do it. You tune out all the fears, things that can go wrong and distractions, and just focus on one step at a time.

Who knows what would have happened to me if I hadn't made the decision to try and climb down the cliff. This was before iPhone's and GPS and I'm not even sure the reception would have worked. Maybe I'd have frozen to death if I had stayed up there, hoping a rescue team would be launched to come find me, but the reality is that it would have been nightfall before anyone realised I was missing, and at that point I'd have been facing a night up there with no food, water or heat.

I have always been a risk taker, but this one was about more than risk; it was about a clear mind, decision making, prayers and luck.

I share this story with you because it relates well to negotiations and decision making, when you break it down. If I hadn't focused on what I wanted and carefully evaluated the options available within the context of the situation I was facing and avoided the red herrings, red flags and distractions, there would have no doubt been an undesirable outcome.

It was critical for me to understand where I was going at all stages of the descent, even when it felt like I was failing. Prioritising my wants in order of preference had informed my actions, based on the context as it changed over time. Any new information was assessed and the order of my priorities changed. For instance, when I first fell flat on my back, my priority was to stop moving. When this failed because I was traveling at high speed, I reprioritised my goals and focused on facing forward, rather than backwards or off to the side. This allowed me to see the oncoming danger and take steps to safeguard myself as best I could. It was this reprioritisation of my wants that, in effect, saved my life. In negotiation, we must understand that as new information appears or circumstances change, so too will the order of our wants. So that it is not just a case of knowing what you want, it's knowing what you want within a specific context at a particular point in time.

Knowing what you want informs the next phase of preparation. This is the due diligence that should be routinely conducted so that you are armed with the facts around you of what's good, average and bad in terms of a deal. If you are negotiating a redundancy package, then you know what an average deal is by knowing what the standard offering is in a typical redundancy. From here you can conduct due diligence to find out what the industry norms are, what your competitors would offer and what colleagues have been offered in the past. This overlays another layer of information and informs the decision-making process, and most importantly, whether you will accept the offer as it is or propose a new package.

3.2 Put Yourself in Their Shoes

As a top negotiator, the more you can engage with the question, what do they want from this negotiation and the more you seek to understand rather than force your way of thinking on the other person, the greater your chances of success. I understand that to some this may seem counterintuitive. After all, this is a negotiation, aren't we supposed to win and get an agreement? Isn't that the point? You'd be right and normal to have these thoughts. However, if you are thinking this way a mindset shift needs to occur as this method of approaching the negotiation is only half the story.

Think of it this way, the other person cares way more about what they have to say, what their motivations are for the negotiation and what they have going on than they do about what you have to say about it. Dale Carnegie said in his widely acclaimed and bestselling book, *How to win friends and influence people*, 'You are intensely and eternally interested in what you want. The only way to interest the other fellow is to talk about what he wants and to show him how to get it.'

Negotiation is about persuasion and influence, and one of the quickest ways to gain influence and make suggestions that will actually have weight when they are implemented and acted upon, is to be liked. Carnegie suggests our aim should be that people will love us, rather than admire us. Admiration, he says, turns into envy, whereas love is a bond that we can have which puts people in the palm of our hand. He suggests the way to be loved is to listen attentively, let the other man speak and let them talk it out. By listening and being a good audience, we actually feed the other person's ego and this feeds neatly into one of the biggest drivers of human psychology. We all want to feel important and we all want to be loved. By making people feel important, we stroke their egos so that they like us more, which turns into love. By listening sympathetically to their needs, we can get closer to understanding their motivations and thereby capture what it is they are really after. This is key to delivering success when negotiating because rather than it being a quest to convince the other person to see it from our perspective, we are able to suggest solutions that will not only suit our needs, but take care of the other person's side as well.

My advice to you is this, put yourself in the other person's shoes before each and every negotiation and honestly try to engage with the question: if I was them, what would I want from this negotiation? Note these points down and seek to understand them when you engage in the negotiation. After all it is their business, so it is arrogant to assume that we know more about their needs than they do.

Carnegie advises us that we should start each interaction with a yes, yes response from the other side. This is achieved by engaging them in a series of questions that get them to respond with yes, yes. In doing so, we create a virtuous cycle in which the outcomes are more favorable. By highlighting what you agree from the start, you draw the other side closer. You show them that agreement has already been found, as opposed to listing off what you don't agree on and then working through each of the issues remaining. Starting out with a no response is a bad strategy because psychological pride gets in the way. Once people have said no, they are inclined to stick to their guns with the no response because it damages their ego if they change to an affirmative agreement. By beginning with yes, we disarm this process. Then, by encouraging them to speak at length and in detail, we show them that we are here to strike a good deal whilst understanding their reasoning, which makes them feel important. It's a winning method of using psychological principles to reach a higher goal by uncovering higher quality wants and needs.

The drivers of success in this field of negotiation are principles that have been taught and spoken of across all walks of life that remain as important today. Henry Ford once said, 'If everyone is moving forward together, then success will take care of itself.' The way I see this, in relation to negotiation, is that if you pick holes in the other side's strategy and take them down and absolutely own them, you don't win. I mean, you'll feel awesome for a short time, but in reality, the other side have lost and that means you lost too because a high level of thinking and understanding was not achieved. Resentment will build up on the other side and you'll never gain their respect. This is important when we think about building long-term valued relationships that can be called upon to achieve great deals. Remember the goal of negotiation isn't to get an agreement, it's to get an outstanding agreement that satisfies both sets of needs.

To summarise, Dale Carnegie's *How to win friends and influence people* highlights 9 ways that will help you to win people over to your way of thinking.

1. The only way to get the best of an argument is to avoid it
2. Show respect for the other person's opinions and never tell a man that he is wrong
3. If you are wrong, admit it quickly and emphatically
4. Begin in a friendly way
5. Get the other person saying yes, yes immediately
6. Let the other man do a great deal of the talking
7. Try honestly to see things from the other person's point of view
8. Let the other man feel that the idea is his
9. Be sympathetic with the other person's ideas and desires

These are superb principles to abide by in the field of negotiation. The possession of people skills and the ability to influence and engage with others are incredible assets that will help you to accomplish solutions that meet your needs and create situations that not everyone is able to attain.

One of the greatest American investors and finance executives, Charles Schwab, describes his ability to influence others and build relationships in this way: 'I consider my ability to arouse enthusiasm among men the greatest asset I possess. The way to develop the best in a man is by appreciation and encouragement'. Applying this sound advice to our own lives and thinking about our negotiations, I hope you are starting to see that there is another way other than confrontation to 'win' in negotiation. By talking about what they want first, it sets the stage for being able to talk about what you want later.

Carnegie uses this example, 'If you don't want your son to smoke, don't preach to him from your point of view but show him that smoking cigarettes may keep him from making the baseball team or winning the 100-yard dash.' Can you see the difference? By focusing on what he wants, we get what we want. It's a subtle but vital change in approach.

3.3 How to Structure a Job Offer Negotiation

If you're like most people, you freak out at the thought of a salary negotiation, but really, what's to fear? This is your opportunity to put an adequate compensation package on the table and, in return, they get all the wonderful things that you will do for the company. They get to unlock and retain all that value, whether it's potential or realised, from day one; don't put yourself down.

Reframe from a distributive mindset to an integrative mindset.

People fear this stage because they are looking at it from the amateur perspective; they fear that if they walk away without the absolute maximum the employer is willing to pay they have somehow lost or missed out.

This type of thinking is detrimental to your negotiation and can ultimately make it hard to find an agreement. The salary negotiation part of a job interview is your opportunity to see how your ideals match up to that of your potential employer. Switching to an integrative approach brings with it numerous benefits, not least the idea of negotiating as a package rather than a series of linear negotiations. When negotiating with either the recruiter or the hiring manager, you need to outline up front all of the elements of the deal that you wish to improve. It's important to put them on the table at the start and indicate which items are of more importance upfront. That way they can go into bat for you and come back with a suitable offer. By indicating your order of preference, you give them the opportunity to go in strong for the elements of the package that matter most to you and are more likely to make you take the job.

If you've done your homework and set it up appropriately for this stage, you will have engaged in sense checking along the various stages of the process with the employer or recruiter so that you will know that you are roughly in the same ball park; now it's just about fine-tuning the deal to make it as sweet as possible for both of you.

Remember they are getting something out of this too – your commitment, blood, sweat and tears for at least the next couple of years. So it's important to be open in this part of the process to allow the best negotiation to take place.

The question is, how do you make the deal as sweet as possible for both parties?

To do this you need to know three things:

1. Your ideal salary figure (this should be about 20% higher than the salary you actually need)
2. Your acceptable say 'yes' salary: 'Happy days, I start work on Monday, where do I sign?'
3. Your 'no-go' figure. If they offer you this, do not pass go; do not collect $200; you won't be taking the job.

To begin with, start with your ideal salary figure and then work your way to your acceptable say 'yes' salary figure. Nine times out of ten the employer will start at the lower boundary of their budget and the employee may start higher. This is a good thing; it means you both know where the goalposts are and the playing field has been established.

Now it's time to listen, ask questions and listen again; this is a key stage of information sharing that will be the foundation of a solid relationship if it's handled in an empathetic and calm manner.

Remember, there are many ways a job package can be structured to offer you benefits that will save you money in the long run, such as health care, car parking, days off, flexible start times, gym memberships, pension contributions, maternity leave, equity and relocation.

By starting out with your ideal salary in mind, and at the same time understanding the employer's perspective (they are paying to get value from you in the future; they are making an investment in you for the future cash flows that you will bring into the business), it's actually a time for bonding and building the relationship.

That's what win-win outcomes are all about; building up long-term sustainable relationships, whether this is negotiating a job offer with HR or negotiation with your gardener. The beauty of this type of goal is that you can have fun with it in the process; by having an honest conversation about the reality of what's on offer, miracles can happen as previously unthought of options unveil themselves.

The employer will have a budget in mind and a vested interest in you at this stage, as you will have too. It's almost like a third date and you're wondering who's going to ask first to take it to the next level and get serious. This is where the skill of real negotiation can take place – the quest to find that sweet spot where mutual benefits are harvested. It's not about beating the other person or extracting way too much out of them, it's about forming a foundation on which a partnership is formed. Like any relationship, it's important to set boundaries and be honest; this is why it's important to get all those awkward questions out of the way. By asking questions and asking for advice from your future employer, they will feel more empathy towards you and more connected, and as a result, will be more likely to help you to overcome whatever is needed to help you make your decision.

One strategy is to ask for their advice; it will actually help to strengthen the relationship. Showing vulnerability is a good thing; it shows you respect the formation of a solid relationship. This is not the time to get all Michael Douglas on them by letting your ego do the talking and slamming the phone down after belting out a shopping list of demands, like he did in the movie *Wall Street*.

This is the time for romance, understanding and flexibility. Using phrases like 'I understand' and 'I'm hearing what you're saying' communicates to the employer that they have been heard; it shows respect and makes it easier to have an open conversation. It is appropriate to show your appreciation and happiness at this stage. Say things like 'I am over the moon' or 'I am really excited about the direction this is going and I'd really like to explore how we can make it work for both parties to move this forward.' These are great bonding phrases littered with positivity that signal, 'I am here, I am open to what you need, and I am willing to work with you to get there.'

The next stage is to state your ideal salary. Don't beat around the bush, just say it, calmly and politely. 'My ideal salary would be $xxx,xxx, based on the market and the level of experience I bring.' It is important that you state *why* you feel you deserve this salary, as the justification allows them to start to believe this too. If you feel that you are worth x, what matters is that also they believe it also. In an ideal world, this conversation would happen once in the very initial stages of the interview process and then again at the final stages when an offer is about to be prepared. That way both parties have the chance to set expectations early before they become financially and emotionally invested. At all stages, you should aim to be likable. This is not the time to act coy or come across as arrogant by waving alternatives in their face or presenting ultimatums. Being liked by HR or the hiring manager will put you streets ahead of the competition. If they like you, they will vouch for you and this, balanced with an appropriate level of rationale to back up your statement, will hold you in good stead.

The thing to keep in mind here is that things change; just because the recruitment budget is $60,000 doesn't mean they won't stretch to $85,000 for someone with your level of experience and ability to hit the ground running. Be prepared to have answers ready for tough questions, like 'Have you got any other job offers currently' or 'What's the lowest salary you would accept.' It's crucial that you don't get offended by these types of questions. It can sometimes come across like they are trying to low ball you or make you feel insecure about your current position, but in reality, the true goal of questions like these may not be so sinister. Often this kind of question is asked because HR is trying to establish if they need to move quickly with the process in order to not miss out on you. Or they are trying to establish how hard they will need to fight internally to get the deal over the line, and if its' worth it based on your enthusiasm for the role. More often than not, the intent of the question is valid but this kind of tough questions like often throw people off their game. This is because they are unprepared for them and interpret them as prying for information that is privileged when in reality the true intention is to help the process. Therefore, I recommend having clear answers to tough questions so that you aren't caught off guard and can give an answer that represents your professionalism and still presents you in a great light to the employer.

Language and the way that you present the information is highly important, so don't second guess yourself, just go for it. At the same time, it's important not to come across as brazen or inflexible.

In the same light, presenting the information as fact, in a harsh tone, could come across as arrogant. Remember, you are still being interviewed and you haven't got the job offer yet. How you manage this process says a lot about you as a person and your ability to have tricky conversations. My advice is to make this part as fun as possible, be honest and help the recruiter or hiring manager to put themselves in your shoes. This way they at least know where your head is at and it's a case of working out how to navigate the difference.

Next, switch it up and talk about other options like equity by asking, 'Is there any opportunity for equity, and how that would work?' This shows you are flexible in your approach and not just fixed in terms of mindset about how you find the sweet spot. Now gauge whether there is no money left in the can. The employer may tell you they only have a certain budget signed off, which absolutely might be true. If they are an efficient business they will have mostly allocated a certain amount of funds towards a specific role; that doesn't mean to say that they won't be willing to be flexible for the right person who adds the right value in experience to the team. You've just got to get them to say it; by remaining calm, keen for the job and positive that you can find a solution, it will naturally come up as a choice.

The other option they might suggest is a salary review after six months once the predetermined Key Performance Indicators (KPIs) are met. This is not as bad as it sounds but do make sure you get it written into your contract with specific amounts and dates before accepting. Getting paid for your results is a superb way to go; not only does it show you back yourself, but also gets you to close the funding gap.

My advice here is to state that you are after a win-win partnership, and by bringing you on board they will receive value in the form of x (inset value, contacts, revenue, skills) coming into the business and, therefore, you are happy to work with them on what the salary looks like, but the market value you are seeing right now is $xxx,xxx.

The employer now has a choice; either hold firm (which might mean there really is no extra cash left in the kitty) or up the initial budget and make you a counter offer. If they hold firm, you can move the conversation on to soft currency benefits that can help you to close the funding gap. If they counter, then you can either accept or propose a new figure. Once you reach a deal, thank them and if possible state that you would like to ask for a salary review after six months for the rest of the gap.

It's all about inching your way along to what a reasonable package looks like for you. Ultimately, it's you that's going to have to work there and you that knows your real market value. Once this has been settled upon, don't then rush through the rest of the package. Take your time, enquire and remain interested happy and upbeat. Get the unknowns out in the open. This is the time to make it a win-win solution, especially when you have shown yourself willing to work with them.

Other soft currency items that often get forgotten in the excitement of an offer are:

- Holiday days (do they increase one per year as a length of service reward)
- Flexible working (start times, hours, working from home or remotely)
- Health care
- Gym memberships
- Bonus (how is this calculated, when is it paid, reviewed, accelerators, caps?)
- Equity (what's the vesting period, price?)
- Parking
- Study programmes (MBA)
- Training (Leadership, Sales, Development)
- International travel (to other markets, offices)
- Expenses
- Conferences (builds brand and knowledge)
- Paid lunch/meals

- Pension contributions
- Corporate discounts
- Start date
- Early Review based on KPI's (6 months, verses a year)
- Visa assistance
- Onboarding Programs
- Opportunities to work with mentors
- Maternity/Paternity leave

Holiday days, flexible start times and health care are just a few of the soft currency perks, but they all matter in the long run, so don't get caught up in the excitement of landing 'the best role ever' just to forget to talk specifics on your bonus. When will it be paid, in what situations might it not be, how is it calculated specifically? This stuff really matters as you don't want to sign up for a role only to find out that you have no way of achieving the targets or the terms are drastically unreasonable.

The more information you can extract at this stage the better; it will give you a larger base from which to make an educated decision about the company you are going to make a commitment to.

After all, if you say yes to this, it inadvertently means that you are saying no to something else. There have been numerous times that I have witnessed people get so excited about the deal they have done on the day of getting a new job, only to find that a couple of weeks later they are thinking about all the things that they really should have put on the table, but didn't think about at the time. Don't be one of them; take your time, plan out what's important and ask the awkward questions.

3.4 Your Ideal, Acceptable and No-go Limits

As a way of dealing with this, take an A3 sheet of paper and divide it into three columns. This works for anything; it doesn't just have to relate to salary negotiation.

Label the three columns:

'Ideal'	'What I really need'	'No-go'

Then, start by writing in the middle column 'what I really need', write down all the things that you really would like in order to feel this was a good deal.

Next, move to the 'ideal column' and write the maximum salary that you think you can achieve in the market, followed by anything else that would be a 'nice to have' but not essential. Your ideal column should be filled with perks that are possible but incredibly sort after. These perks can also be elements that speak to the role itself, such as career advancement, challenge, creativity, financial freedom, wealth, intellectual stimulation, purpose, social value and mentorship.

Finally, go to the no-go column. The questions to engage with here are things like, how low would the salary need to be not to take the job, where is the tipping point, does something else other than salary matter more to you, like flexible working hours. The idea here is to find out where the line is. If it's in your no-go column, it's ultimately telling you what your non-negotiables are.

For example, things that might go here could include a salary below $55k, 15 annual holidays, no career advancement in the next year and office location more than 10km from home. By engaging in this process, you are defining where you want to play so that when you get a job offer, you can see clearly how it aligns with your values, goals and needs.

'Ideal'	'What I really need'	'No-go'
25 Days Annual Leave		15 Days Annual Leave
	$80k	<$55k
	City Location	+15km from home
Car allowance	Parking	No travel allowance

In this task, clarity and specificity are paramount. Imagine that you have the job and then look at it from three perspectives: the perfect world, the real world and a troublesome world. Having a visual sense of what you want will also help you to calibrate when you are in the midst of the negotiation.

If you are conducting the negotiation over the phone, have your A3 sheet out in front of you so that you don't forget anything. The key is to get granular; be specific and confident in your delivery and you will open the door to a world of possibility. By coming to the party prepared, you will position yourself and your potential new employer for success. What will proceed is a calmer, more considered and ultimately aligned conversation that ends up closer to the needs of both parties.

In the event of the conversation stalling, it can be a sign that the employer hasn't prepared fully, in which case go easy on them at first. Give them the chance to go away and research and get back to you. If they don't make a point of clarifying these points, then chase them up. If they still don't come to the party with the information you require, then the conversation may take unnecessary turns and important points will be missed. It may also be a warning sign that you need to think about your priorities a well as whether you want to work for an organisation that takes such a relaxed approach to your questions.

Adopting a growth mindset for this conversation will set you up for success. It will allow you to engage in a process of exchange, bargaining for elements of the deal that are higher up on the priority ladder. You may need to concede on certain points in exchange for others. The goal here isn't to achieve everything on your list; it's to work professionally with the hiring manager to create and inform the process so that more successful outcomes are reached.

Quick Summary

- Know your desired outcome before you go to the bargaining table
- The are plenty of lucrative soft currency benefits to be negotiated in a job offer
- It's your responsibility to know your ideal, needed, and no-go preferences when negotiating. If you haven't done your homework, there is no one else to blame.
- In salary negotiations, always go in at 20% higher as this sets the expectations and allows you to manoeuvre the negotiation from the start.

Activity

Think about how likeable you are and how you currently ask for something that you want. It's a challenge to be objective about this but what I want you to do is identify a real-life negotiation that you need to have in your mind. Write down all the things that you can think of that the other person wants, needs and is driving in the negotiation. Now think of ways that you can articulate what you want whist still coming across as a genuinely nice person. Now go have this negotiation. What did you learn about likeability and getting what you want?

Next, move on to the tough questions outlined below and come up with some well-structured professional answers that present you in a great light as a strong candidate who has integrity without lying or coming across as arrogant.

Tough questions:

1. Do you have any job offers or final round interviews currently?
2. We don't typically pay that salary for this role, so all we can offer is the stated salary. What do you think?
3. How long have you been searching for a job?
4. What is your current salary?
5. What are your salary expectations?
6. Why do you want that salary?
7. Are you interviewing anywhere else?

4

NEGOTIATION PREPARATION

'Fail to prepare, prepare to fail.'
Benjamin Franklin

4.1 Do Your Homework

L IKE ANY GOOD dish, negotiation is a dish best served well prepared. Rush into it without doing your homework and you'll end up running for the door with soup all down the front of your shirt. It's not pretty and it's not world class.

In this chapter, we'll take a look at the things you should consider before getting into a negotiation. Now don't get me wrong, sometimes due to the contextual and practical factors of the situation, it's not possible to do all of these steps before the negotiation is upon you.

But, taking 20 minutes or so to do some research, plan a strategy and identify what it is you ideally want from the deal is worth its weight in gold.

Negotiating is like flexing a muscle; the more familiar you are with the scenarios and contexts that can appear, the bigger they get.

I am a big believer in action, so I am not recommending that you dwell on the negotiation for days. The goal here is to get clarity over what you want out of it and what you are walking into. In most cases, 10-20 minutes of planning followed by action will achieve the desired results. The worst thing you can do is over-prepare or not think about it at all, as there is a subtle balance when planning the negotiation which allows yourself the flexibility to be creative in the moment. Each and every person will have their own threshold as to how much planning they need to do versus how quickly they can get into action. For some it will be 30 seconds, for others it may be a 10-minute ritual. It's a bit like doing the warm up for a workout at the gym. There are some key things that will definitely help and then some things that are nice to have if the situation allows. As you get more experienced in negotiations, you will develop your own routine and it will begin to become second nature, so much so that you may do it unconsciously as you become more expert in your negotiations and experience more success as a result.

Here are some key elements that are useful to identify before going into a negotiation:

1. **Who are you dealing with?** (Status, number of people; what's their negotiation style?)
2. **History of the relationship** (How invested are they in the negotiation? What history do you have with this person?)
3. **What does the other side want from the negotiation?** (Do you know? How sure are you of this? Could there be something else that matters more?)
4. **Time of day** (When will the negotiation take place? Is this the best and most appropriate time?)
5. **Context of the situation** (Are there time constraints or reputational, financial and situational factors that need to be considered?)

6. **Where is the negotiation taking place?** (Are you likely to get interrupted? Is it the ideal place? What can you do to limit disruption?)
7. **What do you want?** (Ideally, plan b, what is the least?)
8. **What are your non-negotiables?** (Are they subjective? If so, replace them, be specific)
9. **What don't you know?** (What is unknown? What isn't it known by both parties?)
10. **What type of negotiation?** (Complex, simple or multiple factor?)

4.2 Know Who You'll Be Dealing With

It's important to understand who you'll be dealing with. There's nothing worse than walking into a negotiation and thinking you are dealing with one person, only to realise that you're dealing with a whole posse and you didn't bring any backup.

To get clarity on this just ask the question: 'Who else will be there, or is it just you?' If possible, try to get all the decision-makers who will need to sign off on whatever is decided in the room at the time of the negotiation. I know what you're thinking; wouldn't they already be there if this was an important negotiation, and you'd be right to think that. That's logical but that's not the way the world works. In reality, it can be slightly different. You might have gone through all of the motions of negotiating and come to an agreement only to find out that the person you have been dealing with doesn't have the authority to sign it off and needs to clear it with their manager.

The best thing to do is to make sure you get yourself into this type of situation. It is actually very damaging. First off, it slows things down; secondly, it reveals your strategy and what you want, ultimately leaving you with less bargaining power when you have to renegotiate with the decision maker.

If possible, always make that sure you are dealing with the decision maker as well.

One-on-one

One-on-one can be one of the simplest and straightforward negotiations around; it can also be one of the easiest to mess up because it only relies on the two people and there are no other parties to mediate if things get tricky, so often the deal falls through before it's even had a chance to begin.

This is the best way to look at it – you have a direct shot at getting the best deal possible for both parties if you are negotiating one-on-one, and of making the process as streamlined as possible.

Key tips to think about before one-on-one negotiating:

- What's motivating the other person?
- What do they want out of the deal?
- What's the history of the relationship? Are they related or have they been referred through a friend or colleague? Have you done business with them for years or is this a completely new relationship?
- How do they usually like to do business?
- What are their expectations?
- What is their understanding of your business, your proposition and of you?
- Do they like you?

That last one is super important. In negotiation, the power of influence that comes from making others like you is incredibly strong. If someone likes you they will be more likely to bend over backwards to help you reach your goal than if they have a strong dislike or are even impartial. The key here is that the 'like' must be genuine (e.g. would you want to spend time with this person outside of the negotiation?). This is why so many deals get done on the golf course, and why having common interests and revealing them can work to your advantage.

The negotiation is about much more than getting the deal done; it's about building your network, your influence and the long-term sustainability of relationships. Remember that we get much of our information from others, so when you think about how someone likes to operate, you get that information from your network or others who've dealt with that person. You don't want people reaching out to their network to ask how you are to deal with, only to find out that you rip people off or only like to 'win' in negotiations.

Two-on-one

This is where things can get a little trickier, through the simple fact that there are two of them and one of you. The way to handle this is to call it out, but don't make it 'a thing'. For example, you could say, 'That's great you're both here – this means we can get the deal done even faster.' The way to approach this is to state your goal upfront. For example, 'I would like to get a better understanding of your business and how we can work together, as well as share with you some of the considerations from my side, and it's great that the two of you are here so that we can all work together to progress this.'

Ultimately, when there are two of them and one of you, so you will need to have your wits about you because they will bounce off each other to speed up the conversation, and use each other to back up what the other is saying (giving the perception that it is true) and be able to pause and reflect while the other is still talking. Whereas for you, it's just you, but don't let this put you off negotiating with more than one person. The important thing is to call it out if things are going south purely because there are two of them.

Key tips for two-on-one

- Don't let the conversation run away with itself
- Ask for further clarification and explanation if you need it
- Don't feel pressured to answer right away; use silence to slow the conversation down and give yourself time to pause and prepare your response
- Tell it how it is; if it's feeling pressured, let it be known and call it out
- Don't feel intimidated; the goal is to work together and if you can find the right momentum, positivity and trust then there is no reason why this can't be the best-case scenario

Negotiating in a team

Often in business, we work as part of a team, and sometimes need to go in as a team to negotiate with another party as part of our jobs. What often happens is, you'll walk into the room and begin conversations with the other side only to find out that you and your work partner aren't on the same page.

It can be anything from the tone and style of the negotiation, to what you exactly want out of it, the amount of time you have to do the deal or even the strategy for successful negotiation.

In truth, there are a lot of variables that need to be worked out in the negotiation preparation stage, rather than in front of the client, where it would be embarrassing and unprofessional to do this and leave value on the table.

Key tips: Factors to discuss with the team (pre-negotiation)

- What success looks like? (What's the agreed ideal outcome? Be specific)
- Who will take the lead?
- What is your style?
- What style is best for this particular negotiation?
- What is your relationship with the other party?
- Are there time parameters?
- What is the walk away point?
- In order of priority, which issue matters the most?

Team dynamics – do you have the right people on the team?

Firstly, it's so important to remove anyone who feels awkward or would seek to discredit the process of negotiation when you're at the negotiation table. Get rid of them now. This might sound harsh, but the truth is you are setting yourself up to fail by not having all team members on the same page. As we know, the negotiation may take many twists and turns, so those who don't believe it's possible will find their ability to stay the course is severely impaired.

These people don't mean any harm; they simply believe the situation is too uncomfortable and believe the outcome to be impossible because they lack skill and experience in negotiation.

Ultimately, this is their own self-fulfilling prophecy playing out; it's exactly because they don't believe it can happen that it doesn't, and they sadly experience less successful negotiations in their lives as a result.

Therefore, it stands to reason that they feel uncomfortable when they are around others while negotiating because of their own experiences. So they end up projecting their own experiences of negotiation onto the situation, which can sabotage the negotiation from the moment it begins.

My advice is to remove these people from the negotiating team. There is no room for pessimism; we want people who will be fully on board from the get-go and believe that it is 100% possible to find an agreement.

As we know, conscious beliefs and unconscious beliefs are incredibly powerful drivers. Tony Robbins, the motivational guru, often talks about how our beliefs influence the level of 'potential' that we see in a situation. This has an impact on the actions people are willing to take and on the result they achieve, 'and then ironically that result, reinforces their belief'. We end up in a downward spiral where the results get weaker and weaker because of this self-fulfilling prophecy.

For example, imagine you are in a restaurant, stood at the counter ready to order food and you say to your friend, 'Watch this, I'm going to see if they'll give us a discount on our meal.' Immediately, your friend reacts by saying 'Nooooooo' and cringing at the thought. This reaction surprises you; after all, you've been reading *The Art of Negotiation* and you want to practice your new-found negotiation skills. In your eyes, this is the perfect opportunity. So, you step up to the counter, make eye contact with the waiter and begin to order food, building up a rapport as you go, engaging fully in the event. At the end of the order you say, 'I don't suppose you could do us a discount?' The waiter looks up from the till. After looking at you, he looks at your friend, who by now has his head in his hands. He is sending off all the wrong signals, rather than supporting you with your positive suggestion of a discount, appealing to the waiter's good nature and optimistic attitude. Your friend is unsupportively signalling to the waiter that this was a bad idea, that you aren't in agreement, and that he is correct to deny your request and that it's okay.

The next thing your friend does is even worse: as soon as the waiter presents their rationale for not being able to give you a discount and you are about to respond, your friend tries to get you to stop, saying: 'No, don't, he said he couldn't do it.'

Your friend will start to almost agree with the waiter, helping him to close the negotiation down. This undermines your initial request and damages both your credibility and position. In this way, they are acting solely on their fear-based beliefs that it can't and won't happen. Therefore, without even realising it, they have caused the negotiation to grind to a halt so suddenly, just as it was beginning to get started.

You, on the other hand, *expected* the waiter to come back with a reason as to why they 'can't offer you a discount'; but you know this doesn't mean that they *won't* give you a discount and you are fully prepared to have that conversation.

Whereas your poor friend gave up before you even got past the first round. In fact, they didn't even want you to get into the ring and have a go. Their beliefs held them back before the negotiation had even begun; that is why you must be so careful about who you have on your team when negotiating as part of a team.

In the above example, it is much harder to deny the request of two enthusiastic, persistent and positive people when negotiating in a team, but as soon as one of them breaks rank, it's all over, and the landslide begins to happen. As soon as one person on the team indicates the opportunity for an 'out' or agrees with the other side in the early stages, you can be sure that the negotiation will rapidly conclude with a less desired outcome.

In a quick-fire negotiation like this, there is a split second where the person being negotiated with needs to make a decision, and it they will look around for reassurance and external signals that they are doing the right thing. They will check you, the situation and your friend, as well as whether their boss is around. All of this happens in the briefest of moments, almost like an assessment or appraisal of the situation. They will make a judgement and then respond. If you and your friend hold your position, just for that moment, it is likely to work in your favour, because you are signalling to them, and to the world, that you believe it should happen.

Tony Robbins says that when we have 'absolute certainty' that something will happen, when we have no doubt in our mind, the potential it has of happening is a given, and we skip right past that stage to taking the actions that are necessary to get the results we want. This is why visualising the results that you want is such a powerful tool, as you are almost thinking your future into existence. By focusing on the result, you are willing it to happen; your beliefs rise and you go all out for it.

Of course, different cultures and upbringings play a big part in why certain people have an aversion to negotiation and will experience less successful negotiation in their lives. For example, if you grew up in a family that believed asking for a discount or haggling on the price was somehow rude or not 'the done thing', then you will carry this with you. Whether you are aware of this or not depends on your motivation to become world class at negotiation. People who have spent time understanding how they truly feel about negotiation will be more aware and, as self-help books tell us, self-awareness is the first step to change. Those that are unaware will go about their negotiations less successfully or even seek to avoid negotiation altogether in their lives because it provokes feelings from their past that are really to do with how their parents viewed negotiation.

In my experience, it takes longer than just one negotiation for someone who carries these beliefs to see that it is possible. Beliefs are deep rooted, especially when they come from our childhood, as they form the foundation and the very basis of our thought processes. However, the great thing is, our thought processes can be changed over time with repeated exposure and retraining. Experts estimate we must reframe the situation in our minds between 30-180 times in order to change the thought process and make it the default thought. Therefore, someone who desires to make a change to their view of negotiation needs to consciously reframe how they feel about the outcome of a negotiation 30+ times before they can begin to see a change.

If you have a 'negative nelly' on your team, don't worry about it. Just remove them from the process before you start, as it will work to your disadvantage if you don't.

Secondly, I believe there is a negotiator in everyone. This is my motto. It is, therefore, vitally important that members of the team who 'don't think it's possible' have the opportunity to have coaching in order to build up their experience of successful negotiation.

Therefore, I suggest that you work closely with them and coach them through the process. You can do this by giving them a more suitable low-risk opportunity to negotiate and learn from. The best experience in negotiation is practical experience. Therefore, if these people have a desire to learn, there is absolutely no reason why they shouldn't be able to become world-class negotiators.

Let me make it crystal clear; the people that I am referring to will sabotage the negotiation purely because they don't believe it is possible. They will interject during the negotiation process because they are driven by their uncomfortable feelings, fear and a desire to prove that it won't work.

There are many variables that influence the direction of successful negotiation and nudge it along the way to the end. All your efforts should be spent on creating the maximum opportunity for success, rather than convincing someone that it *is* possible. After all, why make it harder on yourself?

Negotiations can be subtly influenced by many external factors, like body language, the ease that humour is allowed into the conversation, the flow of the conversation, the environment and what's going on around you. So, the embarrassment of another will only discredit your team and potentially harm the path to successful negotiation.

The successful environment you have created can be reduced and that moment of consideration lost by external factors or your friend jumping in when there is a pause in the conversation and saying, 'Don't worry about it, we don't need a discount.'

One of the biggest factors is other people. They may not be part of the negotiation; they may just be watching and may even be on your team and want you to succeed.

But ultimately, if they're uncomfortable with the process, their behaviour and actions will be counterproductive, even if it's unintentional, and the journey of negotiating will be a bumpy ride.

Even small gestures, such as shaking their head, laughing at you, rather than with you, and hurrying the negotiation along can have a negative impact. (This is a big one, as people who are not comfortable and don't know how silence works tend to want the situation to be over) These people think that once your request is knocked back, that's it, job done, game over; let's pay the normal price and move along.

You don't want these people around you when negotiating because it will hinder the process and make the outcome less positive. Until they are full ready to stay silent, remain non-judgemental and let you do your thing, it's best to keep them away, no matter how much you want them to understand that it's possible, especially if they are friends. There's nothing more frustrating than a friend telling you they think a negotiation won't work and then unintentionally letting their own beliefs externally influence the outcome. It will cause you grief with your friend.

The same goes for work colleagues too. Those who believe that negotiation is completely possible and are on the same page will experience more successful negotiations than those that don't.

It's important to agree upfront the tone of the conversation, what the goal is and who will say what, or introduce which parts.

It's important that you set yourself up for success and do everything you can to control the variables that you have influence over, like the timing, the pace, the speed, the way you start the interaction, and the person you pick to negotiate with.

Personally, I usually prefer to work alone or with one other person for the first part; it helps to cement the relationship and get the ship sailing in the right direction.

Like chefs in a kitchen, the team works together to create a dish, so you and your negotiating partner need to find your rhythm. Working with others can be great as long as the naysayers and the doubters are kept well away.

4.3 Know the Type of Negotiation You'll be Involved With

To be a master, we must think about strategy. The best way to revise for exams at school was to practise past exam papers and types of questions that are likely to appear. The purpose was to prepare us, and the same strategy can be applied to negotiation. You can do this by thinking about what type of negotiation you are likely to be in. This helps us to apply strategy. For instance, if we overlook the fact we are in a time-bound negotiation, and instead choose to focus on multiple issues, we may miss the mark by a long way as we are failing to acknowledge the time pressure that's involved. It's a vital part of our negotiation preparation strategy – get this wrong and the consequences will be dire.

One-issue negotiations

Get in, get out, and get the job done. Focus on the issue at hand, and when the negotiation is done, resist the tendency to rehash old ground. If you negotiated and got what you wanted, there's no need to justify it, explain or do anything that risks damaging the relationship you have built. Say thank you, and if you want to continue the relationship, suggest catching up for lunch. Don't go over the details of the negotiation, especially if it was easier than you thought; just accept that it was easy and move on.

The same goes for making it overly complicated; sometimes, when you are negotiating there is one matter at hand and it's over in a few seconds. That's it, job done.

With one-issue negotiations, have your upper and lower limits in mind. Focus on specifics in your preparation and have an order of priority as to what matters most, so that you can clearly and confidently work your way through the list as it progresses.

By preparing, you are giving yourself a head start, which will be crucial if the other party comes at you with a quick-fire round of questions or asks you directly what's the most important thing. By having these points neatly organised in your mind, you can succinctly articulate the priorities as you see fit. This will make you feel jovial, flexible and keep the negotiations moving at an appropriate pace.

Often with one-issue negotiations, there is a lot of detail that you can very quickly agree upon. It's usually only the specifics that need to be ironed out.

Multiple-issue negotiations

Focus on one issue at a time. Where issues are interlinked, break them down to the extent that you can start making decisions on small pieces of the puzzle. With large, complex deals, it's often easier to start with what you agree on first and then separate all the issues out. That way, you can connect the dots and work out the best order to tackle each issue and what really matters.

Multiple-issue negotiations run the risk of becoming emotionally charged because people get overwhelmed and it adds to the frustration when they don't see progress happening. This is where you need to engage in the mental toughness strategies of the world-class negotiator by controlling your emotions and not letting the external affect your internal decisions.

That is why making ground early is important. By discussing what you can agree on and what's working allows each side the platform to explain what doesn't currently work and how it could work for them.

People love to feel that things are moving forward, so these small wins that are achieved by breaking down the problem will keep the momentum going while the overall picture is still being painted.

It's a bit like painting by numbers. Over time, the picture comes together; you just need to figure out where to start and where to go next, based on the issues' importance and the linkage between them.

One-shot negotiations

This could be at a house auction. You've got one shot to get it over the line and want to take it off the market before anyone else comes along and gets it, but you don't want to pay the reserve. The key to this is emotional energy; you need to get the seller so excited to do a deal and move on they will engage with you on emotion and experience, rather than logic.

Logic says, 'I set this price; I now want this price.' Emotion says, 'We can do a deal. You're looking for a buyer, and hey presto, here I am, ready and willing to take this property off the market and solve your problem. Rather than go through the stressful rounds of auctions and wait it out, let's wrap this up now and get on with our new lives.' Yeah!

People love energy; they love the idea of it and, after all, we are emotionally beings. With one-shot negotiations, just go for it. Don't beat around the bush, go in with all guns blazing and do whatever it takes to make it happen. Send them flowers, take them to dinner, and go the extra mile for that one-shot request.

Time-based negotiations

When time is a factor, it's not always a factor for both parties, so it's important to understand how time is a factor, and who for.

For example, if there is a contract that needs to be signed in order to secure an order by a certain date, time will be a factor.

If the date can move, then who's in control of the date? What happens if they don't sign the contract and you lose the sale?

These are all questions that need to be considered regarding time, including who does time affect the most?

Once you know this, you can figure out what you would do if time wasn't a factor. Knowing this, you have your benchmark. The negotiation can then work in degrees of closeness to your benchmark, depending on your needs that are driven by the time factor.

The question to ask is this: is time really the factor or is it just being blamed so that they can try to get a good deal? It's also a matter of perspective. Think about it this way;

you get to the airport and want a discount on your ticket, but the plane leaves in an hour, so you don't have much time to waste. What you don't know is the plane's only half full and the airline is under pressure to deliver more to their bottom line. By doing this for you, they can get an extra person on board and build your brand loyalty at the same time. The point is, if we assume we know the full story, then we may miss out on opportunities. It's all about how the information is presented, so make it a habit to routinely get it clear in your mind, what it is you don't know and then challenge your assumptions.

Time can be to your advantage. For example, the fact the flight is leaving soon can work for both of you. It might even mean the airline decide to honour your request because they don't have much time to discuss it.

Price-based negotiations

It rarely comes down to price alone; it can be for all manner of reasons, such as ego, likeability, experience, history, background, expectations, upbringing, family, friends, open-mindedness and many, many more. The point is, whenever someone says it's down to price, you need to question whether it really is, as the price gets blamed for a lot of things. Not just because that's the way things have always been done. Never underestimate habits and routine in price-based negotiation. For example, is it really true that your business couldn't give its customers a 25% better deal right now today and still operate with enough profit to keep the lights on? Is it also true that in the right set of circumstances, this type of discounted agreement would make sense?

Price is a common thing to have to negotiate; but the funny thing is, price isn't the only thing you need to take into account. People have been doing deals for centuries, long before the Egyptians were making huge pyramids out of stone, and these deals were based on likeability. Hell, some people even give things away for free. Don't underestimate the power of other factors in price-based negotiation. I bring this up because you should tap into it in a genuine way. When you're told that price is the biggest factor, the next question you should ask is, 'Who for?' Is it for the person that's getting the sales commission? Yes, definitely. Then wouldn't it be better for them to get a sale, rather than no sale at all? Well, this depends on how much they need to sell. If it's their last item, they'll be reluctant to sell it for less than the typically price unless you can give them something more, that speaks to them as a person. Like introducing them to your network (including more potential buyers) or recommending them for a job.

If price really is the main objective, then stating this up front doesn't always get you the best deal, as people become blinded by it and forget to look out for all the cues and clues that the other side are giving that could help you to get a lower price.

By focusing so much on the low price, they may not get it, or if they do, it comes with a string of caveats that couldn't be considered a 'good deal'.

My honest advice on price-based negotiations is to go in with a sensible, yet commercial proposition and state your expectation. For example, I expect a 20% discount for this deal, 60-day payment terms and blah, blah, blah. You get the idea. Stating this upfront, when we are talking business and there's still excitement in the room, is a strategically advantageous idea. It puts it on the table and makes your requests easier to manage at the time. If you don't, and bring them up later, they can feel like an afterthought.

When you are presented with a contract that states what you asked for; thank the other party for putting it together, and then ask if there's the opportunity for a few more percentage points to be taken off 'because if there could be, then you see a really opportunity for traction in the market,' and reiterate how this will *benefit* them as a business.

Then, when the deal is done and you are up and running, call them to say thank you for putting the deal together. This goes a long way and shows you care about the effort they went to in order to make the deal come to life.

This is the strategy that I recommend, as opposed to hammering on about price. Although price was still an issue in the other example, there was much more value created, compared to the price is king strategy that leaves so much undiscovered. After all, the objective of negotiation is to create maximum value and part of that includes the strong bond that can be formed with the counterparty through the creation process of crafting a superior deal together. If the negotiation becomes fixated on one element, it is hard to describe the full extent of the opportunity available because it remains unexplored. This is rather like driving down one road in a city and then trying to describe what it's like; it's difficult to describe the whole place when you've only seen one street.

6.4 Ask the Right Questions

There are a number of highly useful questions one must ask before going into any type of negotiation. These cover the context, the reality, the history and who else is going to be around. Questions like this might seem a tad trivial, but actually they play a major part in successful negotiation.

Who's going to be in the room?

It's not always possible to find out who will be in the room with you at the negotiation table, but if you can get an idea of the set up beforehand, it comes in mighty handy. This is not only useful from a pre-negotiation visualisation perspective, but also to find out what and who you are up against. In business negotiations, you can often get a scenario where you are dealing with one individual. You discuss the negotiation in depth (probably over the phone), feel it out, define the boundaries and even go through the various stages of the negotiation bargaining process, but then you hit a road block and it's suggested that meeting up is the best step to take. You rock up either at their place or yours and you go into the room to continue the conversation. Then, out of nowhere, their boss or someone with more authority appears and proceeds to take over the negotiation like a bullet train. You realise you are being railroaded, as they straight away start to explain in detail all the reasons why they cannot do what you want. You might as well sit back and relax because you will be listening to a barrage of words for the next few minutes as they outline extensively what's going on for them.

What's happening here is the negotiation has been delegated to a more senior person. You must be prepared for this and think about the possible steps that the other side might take to make the negotiation more favourable towards them before you go to any face-to-face meeting.

Sometimes delegating the negotiation to another person can be a great relief, especially if a level of tension or emotional confrontation is added to the mix. However, it can also be an attempt to press reset on any of the negotiation steps that have previously happened. It's more common to see this type of negotiation strategy play out in a retail environment because there's typically a hierarchical business structure, with the manager at the top having decision-making power over deals, discounts and freebies.

In negotiations like these, you will only get so far. You may even get what you're after and then they will turn around and say, 'I'll just get my boss as they'll need to approve this.' The boss will come in with limited, or 'perceived to be limited', amounts of information about the situation and quickly list off all the reasons why it is not possible (as a demonstration of confidence). This is not a situation you want to be in, so that is why asking the right questions upfront is crucial; so that you won't get yourself into this less than ideal predicament.

Who is the decision maker?

The questions to ask upfront are: 'Are you the manager?' 'Who has the authority to do this?' and 'Who do I need to speak to?' They are important as these questions streamline the conversation.

When you have developed a relationship with someone the negotiation may well need to take various forms and get sign-off at different levels as it progresses. Patience and perseverance are the key traits of any successful negotiator. To be the best, you will need to have both in droves. It's about being able to go a number of rounds with one party and then stand back up again and do the same thing with the next.

In cases where you do find yourself being railroaded by a manager who picks up the conversation and then lists out all the reasons why you can't get a deal across the line, it's best to stay humble and keep your cool. As frustrating as it is to have the 'back to square one' button pressed, it is a part of negotiation, so be prepared to face this quite frequently. This is an area where anger can flare up, as the deal was so close to getting done, you could almost smell it, and now it feels like it's been snatched away from you. It's not surprising you get annoyed at the new state of play, but you must remember that this isn't the truth. What we are aiming for here is the ability to negotiate in any situation, including annoying ones. This is when it's important to hold your nerve, rein in your emotions and have the grit to push through. We'll talk more about emotions later.

The way to handle this is to break the deal down into bite-sized chunks. It is like the old saying, 'How do you eat an elephant? Bit by bit, piece by piece.' You need to take the conversation back to the fundamentals of the relationship and the mutually beneficial reasons for doing the deal. Once the manager has done their thing and given their spiel, acknowledge what they have said by using active listening and repeating what they have said back to them. This demonstrates that you have heard them and shows them respect. This doesn't, however, mean that you agree with what they are saying; it just means that you have heard them. Remember this is only their side of the story, and by acknowledging that you have heard it, you are opening up the conversation to explore your side. Say something like, 'So, is there anything else I need to get from your side to understand where you guys are at?' Or you could say: 'No, OK, cool. Do you mind if I share with you where we're coming from?'

This moves the conversation back into negotiation territory; there may be a way forward you might not be able to see yet. By continuing on, rather than giving up just because the negotiation seems to have hit a restart point, you are increasing the chances of getting closer to what you want.

What is the context of the negotiation?

On top of all of this, it's incredibly important to understand the context of the situation when negotiating. For example, who else is around? Is their boss in the room? Do they need to impress their boss? Try to put yourself in their shoes. Is it their first week in the job and are they under pressure to deliver incremental value as justification for the new role? This is where open questions help you to uncover and elicit new information that may give you a clearer picture of the context.

Is their girlfriend, boyfriend, friends or family watching? If so, these other witnesses will influence the way in which the negotiation proceeds. Being aware of this and who else is around or involved will help you to understand how you can use this to your advantage.

It's not a case of manipulation, it's a case of understanding the situation and whether this it is the ideal moment to strike a win-win deal. If not, it may be better to hold off and wait for a more appropriate setting. If the deal absolutely needs to be closed now, then bring them in closer with humour. You will find that acknowledging the elephant in the room can take the pressure off.

So say something like this: 'I understand we've got an audience [elephant and humour], I also understand that you want to get a deal away [reframing and understanding] and I'd really like that too [demonstration of possibility]. We just need to make the numbers work [the how].'

Negotiation is a process and the language we use is a vehicle that gets us to our destination. By utilising language and asking the right questions, we will streamline the conversation in a way that brings the other side with us, rather than alienating them.

4.5 Open and Closed Questions

The quality of the information you receive is one way to improve your ability to negotiate. As they say, knowledge is power and by understanding the difference between open and closed questions, and when to use each of them, we can become a force to be reckoned with.

Be careful of *closed* questions, such as: 'Can you do a discount?' This only provides the opportunity for one of two answers – 'yes' or 'no'. Whereas, 'What kind of discount can you do?' gives room for a much more open response. The easiest way to remember the difference between open and closed questions is this: open questions start with What, Why, When, Where and How, and their purpose is to uncover information. Closed questions begin with Can, Do, Are and Is, and their purpose is to confirm information.

Open

What is your process for doing that?
How do you feel about that?
When would you like to meet?
Where is the opportunity for you to develop?
Why does it need to be finalised by next week?

Closed

Can we do a deal?
Do you have the time?
Are you in this for the right reasons?
Is this your first negotiation?

Using both questioning styles to uncover and confirm information is a tactical strategic skill that requires practice if it is to be done effectively. The beauty of this questioning style is the quality of the information that it yields and the speed at which you can change the pace of the negotiation. We are only as good as the information that we receive and this is driven by asking the right type of questions. If you aren't receiving either the answer or information you want, have a look at the type of questions you are asking. Are they open or closed, and is this the appropriate style for the purpose you are trying to achieve?

4.6 Get Real With Yourself

There are times when a bit of introspection is needed, as it enables us to be real with ourselves and the situational reality.

Key questions that you must ask yourself include: 'How badly do I need this deal to go through?' A question like this, if answered honestly, helps to define your upper and lower boundaries. Only you can be the judge of what's appropriate; however, sometimes we need to level up and get real, so that we can prioritise what's important.

Here's another one: 'What's the history between you?'

These types of questions require subjective analysis, but it is your ability to be real to yourself and look at something minus the biases, hopes and wishes, and just understand what is actually going on, that will determine how successful you can be at negotiation.

For example, if you want to negotiate the salary for a new job but you are unemployed and need to pay the rent, how much does an extra $5k actually matter, and is it worth losing the job over? If you aren't honest with yourself and have not worked out a systematic prioritisation system to help you identify what's more important, you will end up negotiating for your life goals at all the wrong times.

Quick Summary

- Take time to plan for the negotiation
- Debrief after the negotiation
- Increase the number of variables in team-based negotiations, and be clear on who's taking the lead, what success looks like and what the order of your priorities is.
- Open vs. Closed questions: know when it is appropriate to use each of these questioning styles.

Activity

For the next seven days, I want you to take note of your automatic assumptions about negotiation, and then challenge them. Keep a journal of what you assume and what you know as a fact. Then write down how you are going to reframe your assumptions in a way that gives you unlimited possibility.

The goal of this exercise is to gain a better understanding of what your tendency is to assume details. In this way, you can apply an optimistic mindset to each opportunity that you have for negotiation in your daily life.

By doing this over time, your expectations of the outcome will shift, and as a result, you will see there are more options available than just your automatic default. Sir Richard Branson is a big advocate of carrying a notebook wherever he goes, so that he can jot down his ideas, thoughts and concepts as he goes about his daily life.

Why not create this practice in your own life? By consciously engaging with a journal each day, we allow ourselves the opportunity to reflect and broaden our sphere of understanding.

PART 3

IN THE NEGOTIATION ROOM

5

NON-VERBAL COMMUNICATION

'My mind's telling me no, but my body,
my body's telling me yes.'

R Kelly

5.1 It's Not Just What We Say

IN THIS CHAPTER, I will help you to understand your pattern
of non-verbal communication and show you how it can
either damage or support the negotiation process. I'll also
show you how to read and interpret the other sides body
language so that you will know what the most important cues
are to hone in on during negotiation and how the experts do
it. We will take a look at expanding yourself awareness after
this and the things you can do to increase this awareness
in relation to your team. Non-verbal signalling, heightened
self-awareness and an acute ability to read others are all
critical skills that an expert negotiator needs to master.

The animal kingdom is full of examples of how non-verbal
communication, and particularly body language, is used to
influence outcomes. For example, male peacock's want to
impress the females during the mating ritual (bet you didn't
expect to find a piece on male peacocks and mating in a book
on negotiation but read on, champion) and gather as a group
to engage in a performance called 'leking'. This is a form
of non-verbal signalling and the male hopes to influence a

positive reaction from the female by fanning his tail feathers and strutting purposefully around.

Interestingly, the majority of female peacocks choose a small sample of alpha peacocks to reproduce with. This process in the animal kingdom demonstrates that what we put out to the world has the ability to influence outcomes.

Even the king of the jungle, the lion, goes out of its way to let others know who's the boss. Lions are assertive creatures and use their facial expression and body language to show how they are feeling. They make themselves appear bigger when they feel under threat. This is done by hunching their backs, lifting their tails and standing on tiptoes to give the illusion that they are bigger. They also make sure their teeth and claws are finely on display and ready to go.

It's not much different in the human world. From an early age, we become experts in reading other people's facial expressions and body language, especially those who we are closest to. We are a social species and rely heavily on our judgements to keep us safe and away from danger and to work out the pecking order. Have you ever been to a meeting where two or three senior people try to one up each other. That's the pecking order being worked out, right in front of your eyes.

When it comes to negotiation, however, it can be strategically advantageous to control our emotions, so that the other party does not see our natural reaction. So it's best that we don't immediately start screaming the place down and celebrating if we strike an exceptional deal or react with anger if the deal is going south.

5.2 Facial Expressions

It takes commitment and repeated practice to become a world class negotiator. It's not easy to withhold fleeting micro-expressions. In fact, research has demonstrated that they are uncontrollable for a small portion of time (1/30 milliseconds). Research indicates that micro-expressions occur because there are two neutral pathways that mediate facial expression in our brain. However, when we are involved in intensely emotional situations and need to control our expressions (like high stakes negotiations), we activate both systems at once. This engages the brain in a neural 'tug of war' over the control of our face, and allows for the leakage of micro-expressions that only appear for a fraction of a second before they are overridden by our intended facial expression (Matsumoto and Hwang, 2008; Rinn, 1984).

Micro-expressions as opposed to macro-expressions (which last from 0.5 to 4 seconds) are typically associated with deception and lying, and signify concealed emotions. Porter & ten Brinkle (2008) identified in their paper, *Reading between the lies,* that 'relative to genuine emotions, masked emotions were associated with more inconsistent expressions and an elevated blink rate'. In essence, micro-expressions occur when we attempt to use our emotional expression to be deceitful, which display our true emotion. Interestingly, this research also found that 'negative emotions (sadness, anger, disgust, fear) were more difficult to falsify than happiness'.

Improving our ability to read other people's emotions helps us in a number of real-world ways, like building constructive relationships. Matsumoto and Hwang (2008) state that:

> 'reading facial expressions of emotion, and especially micro-expressions, can aid the development of rapport, trust,

and collegiality; they can be useful in making credibility assessments, evaluating truthfulness and detecting deception; and better information about emotional states provides the basis for better co-operation, negotiation, or sales'.

As world-class negotiators, this is interesting to us. Here is a specific skill that can help us with the foundational building blocks of effective negotiation. Researchers conclude that even though it is highly encouraged, there are significant career benefits to obtaining expertise in this skill and there is ample training and resources to help us improve our ability to read emotional facial expressions, the real skill is knowing when to 'call it out' and when to adapt our own behaviour and communication style to help others. Hypersensitivity towards non-verbal behaviour, including leakage and micro-expressions, can also have an adverse effect on a relationship and damage the rapport that has been built up if we come across as overbearing, intrusive and insensitive by pointing out someone's leaked micro-expression. Knowing what the situation needs, as opposed to simply acting on the basis of knowledge, is one of the many areas where emotional intelligence earns its stripes in negotiation and interpersonal relationships. Matsumoto and Hwang (2008) report that the 'improved ability to read facial expressions, or any non-verbal behaviour, is just the first step. What one does with the information is an important second step in the process of interaction'.

5.3 Body Language

Now I want to introduce you to Amy Cuddy, a behavioural expert superstar. She is an American social psychologist, Assistant Professor in the Negotiation, Organization & Markets unit at Harvard Business School, and known for her work on non-verbal behaviour. Amy is also famous for giving a remarkable TED Talk on the subject of body language that I highly recommend you to watch. This is a TED Talk to watch if you are serious about becoming a world-class negotiator. Did I mention you should watch this TED Talk?

https://www.ted.com/talks/amy_cuddy_your_body_language_shapes_who_you_are

In this talk, Amy explains how changing our posture, even if it's just for two minutes, has the potential to significantly impact the way that our life unfolds. She says we must 'pay attention to what we are doing'. Whether it is hunching, crossing our legs or holding our arms, we are sending out powerful signals to the world.

As humans, each of us makes second-by-second judgements on the world that we experience. This can be anything from who we date, who we hire or even who we avoid in the bus queue.

We are also being constantly influenced by the body language of others and calibrating our own behaviour, while making judgements about the intentions, feelings and social status of others.

In the high stakes world of negotiation, body language is speech through actions. Get this wrong and you're going to have a hard time convincing anyone to do anything. If your body language doesn't match up to what you are saying, then you are going to come across as shady, untrustworthy and awkward. From the moment you make eye contact, judgements and inferences are being made, and if the other person sees you before the initial contact takes place, this will factor into their estimation of you as well. So if you are seen standing in the reception, look nervous before the meeting or stumble on your way to the table, this will all be taken into consideration.

First impressions count; in fact, a first impression is formed in the first seven seconds of meeting someone, psychologists have found. This means what we do to influence or control how we feel before going into the negotiation, as well as what we project outwards, can have a huge impact on the results that we achieve.

Amy tell us that humans are much like the animal kingdom, which expresses power by expanding. Think of Mick Jagger or Jimmy Hendrix on stage, or Usain Bolt celebrating in the power of the moment, she says. Think of boxers when they first come into the ring, beating their chests and strutting around, projecting both their confidence and dominance outwardly.

In contrast, we automatically make ourselves smaller when we feel powerless by retracting our bodies inwards, bowing our heads and pulling our arms and legs towards the centre of our body.

The question that Amy set out to answer was, 'Do our non-verbals govern how we think and feel about ourselves?' In essence, 'Can we fake it, until we make it and how strong is the mind's influence over the body?'

What she found out was that we, as humans, have the ability to express certain behaviours that make us feel happier and more powerful. 'When we smile, we feel happy, but also when we are forced to smile, it also makes us feel happy. It works both ways.'

Amy wasn't done and wanted to find out more about how our behaviours can influence our minds. She wanted to test this out at a hormonal level, so she set up an experiment in which participants either displayed a high-power pose or a low-power pose for two minutes.

What she discovered was game changing. Those who took on the high-power pose – with their arms behind their heads and their body spread out, expanding – were 86% more likely to gamble, when given the opportunity.

In contrast, only 60% of the low-power poses group (with hunched, bowed heads) would gamble, if given the opportunity. But hold on a minute, let's take this one step further –what about on a hormonal level; was there any change there?

Surely, a two-minute exercise in power posing could not have much of an effect, could it? Oh yes, it could. Saliva samples taken from each participant revealed that those in the high-power pose group experienced a 20% increase in testosterone (the hormone associated with assertiveness and risk tolerance).

Whereas those in the low-power pose group experienced a 10% decrease! If that's not saying something, I don't know what is. Not only did posing for two minutes (forced behavioural change) have an effect on the participants' risk-taking tolerance (mindset), it also had a significant effect at the hormonal level (biological).

What about cortisol? You know, the stress-related hormone that goes surging around the body whenever we feel under threat?

Well, it turns out that power posing has a dramatic effect on this as well. Those in the high-power group experienced a 25% decrease in cortisol, whereas those in the low-power group experienced a 15% increase! So, this tells us that power posing, even for two minutes, can help us to remain cool, calm, collected and mentally clear, with the ability to think due to the decrease of cortisol.

Amy states: 'Hormonal changes configure your brain to be either assertive, confident and comfortable or really stress reactive and feeling shut down. So, it seems that our non-verbals do govern how we feel about ourselves.'

Man, this stuff is good. If you're not already Googling: 'Amy Cuddy Body Language', then do it now. This TED Talk is worth 21 minutes out of your life, I promise.

This chat about body language comes into play when you are taking part in negotiations in a big way. Think about all the situations where a decrease in cortisol would be preferable: job interviews, pitches, even when your negotiating the traffic while driving the kids to school. This research and its application in the real world really comes to the fore in evaluative situations like presentations, where your performance is consciously being assessed.

Okay, for those of you who didn't bother to watch Amy's video (which will be minimal because I know you are all highly committed to the pursuit of building the skills required for successful negotiation), I'll explain what Amy talks about next.

Amy conducted another study, which was this time focused on evaluation and how other people viewed the two conditions (high-power pose/low-power pose). Subjects were brought back into the lab and judged and recorded during a high-stress job interview. Judges had been trained to give no non-verbal feedback. Imagine that, you're being interviewed for a job and the interviewer just sits there giving nothing away, not even a smile. Awks!

Following this, a different group reviewed the tapes and the results were astounding. They all wanted to hire the high-pose group because of the presence they brought, and not for the content of what they said. Amy states the judges' reason was that these people were 'authentic, comfortable and captivating'. She continues, 'when people are bringing their true selves to the situation, they bring ideas but as themselves'.

What I want you to get from this is that it's the same situation with negotiation. We must be ourselves at every stage of the negotiation. That doesn't mean, however, that we don't feel anxious or nervous before, during or after it.

What it means is that we must do everything within our control to influence what we project out to the world by leveraging knowledge and acting on research like this. In the negotiations going forward, make sure that you follow the high-power pose technique so you will be able to capitalise on its value and reap the benefits it bestows on your mental processes. It will reposition your thoughts so that they can influence your behaviour and enable you to achieve the outcomes you desire.

Here's Amy again to recap: 'Bodies, can change our minds, and our minds can change our behaviour, and our behaviour can change our outcomes.'

Boom! Well said, Amy.

5.4 The Johari Window

The next technique I want to introduce is called the Johari window. This tool increases our awareness of how we can improve our negotiations in the context of how we come across to others and our relationships with them. It was a technique first created by Joseph Luff and Harrington Ingham back in 1955 and its purpose was to help individuals better understand their relationship with themselves and with others.

Johari Window

	Known to self	Not known to self
Known to others	Arena	Blind Spot
Not known to others	Façade	Unknown

Subjects were told to pick a number of words to describe themselves from a list of 56 potential adjectives (see table below). Then, the subjects' peers were told to do the same thing, picking an equal number of words to describe the person in question. The chosen words were then inserted into the grid, based on the following criteria for each window.

- **Arena:** what is known by both self and by others (e.g. words that they both chose).

- **Blind Spot:** what is unknown by self, but not known by others (e.g. words the peers chose).
- **Façade** – what is known by self, but not known to others (e.g. information we keep hidden – words chosen by the subject and not by their peers).
- **Unknown** – what is unknown by self and by others.

Able	Accepting	Adaptable	Bold	Brave	Calm	Caring	Cheerful
Clever	Complex	Confident	Depend-able	Dignified	Empathetic	Energetic	Extroverted
Friendly	Giving	Happy	Helpful	Idealistic	Independent	Ingenious	Intelligent
Introverted	Kind	Knowledge-able	Logical	Loving	Mature	Modest	Nervous
Observant	Organised	Patient	Powerful	Proud	Quiet	Reflective	Relaxed
Religious	Responsive	Searching	Self-assertive	Self-conscious	Sensible	Sentimental	Shy
Silly	Spontaneous	Sympathetic	Tense	Trust-worthy	Warm	Wise	Witty

Now, I am not for one second suggesting that you sit down at the negotiating table and pull out your Johari window to figure out what vibes the other side are getting from you. That would be ludicrous. But it is useful for expanding our self-awareness and gives us insight into how we come across to others.

This framework is also especially useful in helping us to understand other members of our negotiating team. A team that works together to reduce the blind spot, unknown and hidden areas, will be stronger and more effective as a result. This is a habit that we, as world-class negotiators, should get into on a regular basis, so that we can aspire to increase the size of our arena, both for ourselves and for our team-mates.

Increasing the arena

There are specific ways to increase the size of the different windows. For example, feedback from others is one way to increase the size of the arena, as it increases our self-awareness and reduces the blind spot.

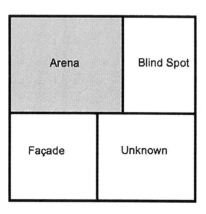

Another way to increase the size of the arena is through the disclosure of information. This seeks to decrease the size of the façade by revealing information. In negotiation, it is the type behaviour that can be used as a strategy to build trust, as it reveals previously unknown details about ourselves to the other person.

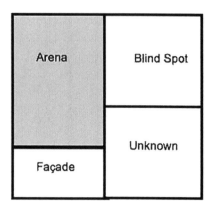

Increasing the façade

The unknown window can be reduced by self-discovery; activities like meditation and travel are perfect for this, as they increase the size of the façade. You can start to see that as we change one dimension, it affects another. Working with others, requesting feedback and focusing the team's energy on reducing the unknown area through an increased observation of self gives us a strategic advantage in negotiation.

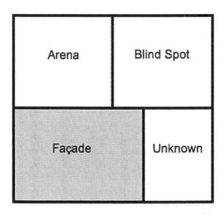

This depiction of the Johari window is great for getting to know new people on a team, or finding out if we are failing to use team-mates' strengths to their full potential. In this example, feedback isn't being shared with the individual at the same time, nor is the individual revealing key details about their abilities. Compounding matters further, there is a relatively large unknown window. A shift in awareness can transform this picture through a process of self-disclosure, self-exploration and consistent feedback.

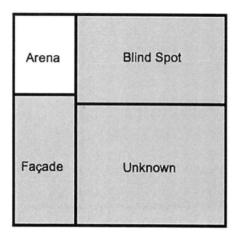

The reason why the unknown area reduces is very important because it relates to effectiveness in negotiation. We could be in possession of the skills that we don't know we have, due to a previous lack of opportunity, limited experience or insufficient exposure to stimuli. Through the very act of understanding this concept, we allow ourselves to be more open to the possibility that there is more to be discovered about our unique talents and abilities. We may also underestimate ourselves. The Johari window allows the feedback of others to be included in the process, which can increase both our confidence and our awareness of our own abilities.

5.5 Emotion and Negotiation

For a long time, research failed to look at the relationship between emotion and negotiation. It wasn't until the mid-90s that psychologists decided to focus on the role of specific emotions, like disappointment, anxiety and anger, and their effect on successful negotiation. Prior to this, research had focused on the transactional elements of deal making, which primarily involves tricks and tactics that massage the negotiation along.

It is funny that it took so long to explore this area of psychology in more detail, as the way we go about creating value together, overcoming obstacles and working through disagreement is heavily influenced by emotions and our response to them. Once we spend some time understanding the role that emotions play and have a clearer picture about the emotions we are displaying, we can learn to control them.

Emotions like anger, sadness, anxiety and disappointment all play out in very interesting ways when they are mixed with the field of negotiation. It has been well documented that the 'fight' response is linked to anger and the 'flight' response to anxiety. In fact, when we dissect the stages of negotiation, we can categorise the propensity of certain emotions to appear at different stages. Emotions, such as anxiety, are typically associated with the pre-negotiation stages and the very beginning when negotiation has only just begun, whereas anger is more prevalent during the middle phase when things can flare up if the negotiation doesn't look to be going according to plan. Disappointment and sadness are usually focused towards the latter stages (closing).

I prefer to negotiate when I am excited, as I find that I get better results and this emotion allows me to overcome any apprehension about the negotiation before it starts, which carries me through the difficult stages where anger or disapproval may occur.

It is important to recognise that we are bringing these negotiations to the table and by understanding when these emotions are likely to occur and the undesirable effects they can have on deal-making, we can start to minimise the risks caused by their appearance.

Anger

Anger is destructive in negotiations, as it acts like a bomb. Not only does it make it very difficult to achieve a win-win deal, it damages the long-term nature of the relationship. In business, we are looking to make long-term relationships and the world is getting smaller by the day through LinkedIn, Facebook and the pace of global connectivity.

In contrast, intimidation, leverage and threats only undermine a person over the long term. I have seen this tactic used only a handful of times in negotiation, as there is no place for threats or leverage as a means to make deals. It is not only undermining and unpleasant, as people like to work with people they like, but others will come to expect this response from you over time and, therefore, anticipate ways around it.

It's a basic strategy and not one that I recommend. It is also worth remembering that we reveal key details when we're angry; it's like Sonic the Hedgehog dropping all his rings when touched by the baddies. So much information is revealed it can be detrimental and make it hard for you to regain control. The other concern is that trust will be dissolved. Displays of anger in the form of outbursts only undermine the relationship and make it harder for real long-term value to be created.

Anxiety

On the flip side, anxiety also has a negative impact on negotiation. When Maurice Schweitzer and Alison Brooks conducted a series of experiments in 2011 they specifically looked at the role of anxiety. They found that people who experience anxiety in negotiation, compared to those who don't, are more likely to make weaker first offers, exhibit lower expectations and generally exit the negotiation earlier.

Damn, that's an awful trio of outcomes, so it's time to ditch anxiety and look forward to successful negotiations instead.

To give you some insight into how Schweitzer and Brooks did this (if you're like me, you'll want to know all the details), 136 participants in one of the studies were tasked with negotiating a mobile phone contract across a range of dimensions, including factors such as the purchase price, warranty and contract length. In a twist, half of the sample was played music from the film *Psycho*, in order to induce anxiety, and the other half was not.

The importance of managing anxiety during negotiation is right there in the results of research. The great thing is that it's clear anxiety in negotiation can be overcome through experience. So if you currently feel anxiety while negotiating, you won't always feel this way.

What I want to make clear in this book is that negotiation is a fun experience; in fact, the times when I feel most alive I feel is when I'm negotiating (well, that and extreme sports). What I find is that negotiations can sometimes get amped up by the individual before they've even begun. They start to think about it and play out what will happen if the deal goes through or what will happen if it doesn't. All of this increases anxiety and hinders performance. If you find yourself over-analysing a negotiation after you've done all the prep work – so that you know your facts, as well as what you want – then my advice is to get on and do it. Just go for it, rather than sitting around magically dreaming up outcomes.

OK, I hear you say. So, I get that anger and anxiety are damaging to the negotiation, Tim, but what if I visibly express signs of anxiety during a negotiation; can I phone a friend?

Well, as luck would have it, researchers have investigated that too in a series of eight experiments. They were keen to find out how anxious people behaved when they had the option to seek advice from others, and what they discovered was that anxious people are less confident and more likely to consult others for advice.

Interestingly, anxious people were more likely to take advice from people who had a conflict of interest in the negotiation, whereas non-anxious participants looked at the advice sceptically. On top of that, the anxious group agreed 12% less financially beneficial deals than the neutrals. Think about it; 12% is a lot of over the course of a lifetime, considering the number of negotiations we encounter on a daily basis.

The reason it's important to get comfortable with negotiation goes back to *The Wall Street* version of negotiation I mentioned earlier. There are some people out there who will try to make you anxious on purpose. They want to see if they can rattle you, and will use this as a tactic to get what they want because they know you're going to be easier prey if they can make you anxious, and will get a 12% better deal.

My number one tip for dealing with anxiety is to breathe deeply. Just pause and breathe. When a *Wall Street* type negotiator tries to work this tactic on you, don't respond or let anything slip out. Just pause and take a breath. By doing this you are giving yourself time, and more importantly, regaining control. You're pulling the negotiation back towards you and onto an equal footing. By not responding too quickly, you're less likely to say the first thing that pops into your head. You're also showing the person that these tactics won't work on you, which will steer the rest of the negotiation away from their anxiety-provoking tactics.

You may have seen the shows *Dragons' Den* or *Shark Tank*, where entrepreneurs eagerly pitch their newly-fledged businesses to a panel of high profile celebrity investors in front of a large studio audience with the hope of getting funded. The producers cleverly intensify the negotiation by creating an environment in the studio that makes it harder for the entrepreneurs. This is done by playing dramatic, anxiety-provoking music and staging the event in front of a large audience.

If you watch the show, you'll no doubt have seen the difference between the anxious entrepreneurs and those who are the least rattled; they negotiate carefully and deliberately. They know their company's value, are able to recall all the key figures and know what outcome they want from the investors.

Now focus on the Dragons. I want you to watch how they raise the anxiety levels in the room and use each other to make counter offers. They do this by dangling the opportunity of funding in front of the founders, trying to make them sweat. It's the entrepreneurs who are able to keep cool in this intense environment that successfully run the gauntlet and appear victorious at the end.

Perception, as they say, is the co-pilot to reality, and one of the big skills in negotiation is being able to tune into your own and others' feelings. Being able to read the situation and understand what's needed next is highly advantageous.

5.6 Courage Case Study

Bethany Hamilton

The next example is Bethany Hamilton, a surfer from Hawaii, whose left arm was bitten off by a 14-foot (4.3m) Tiger shark when she was just 13 years old. On the morning of 31 October 2003, Bethany and her friends went to Tunnels Beach, Kauai, for a morning paddle, like they had done hundreds of times before. Everything about it resembled a normal morning as Bethany made her way out to the break, with one arm dangling in the water. Then, all of a sudden, everything went black.

By the time she arrived at hospital, she had lost 60% of her blood. Bethany's father was due to have knee surgery that afternoon, but it was his daughter who took his place on the operating table that day.

Bethany reported feeling normal at the time of the bite and felt numb on the way to the hospital. The shark had severed her arm just under the shoulder.

Remarkably, only one month after the attack, she was back in the water again, learning how to surf with one arm and training. Two years on, she won first place at the Explorer Women's Division of the National Scholastic Surfing Association National Championships and is now a professional surfer and still taking first place to this day.

That is grit; that is true commitment and doing whatever it takes to practice the thing you love doing the most. It is this level of obsession that leads to excellence. Having the courage and the stamina to keep going despite what is thrown your way; that's what makes a huge difference in this world.

Bethany Hamilton's Lessons:

1. **Let nothing stand in the way of you and your goals** – if you want it badly enough and are willing to be courageous, you will reach your destination. We only fail when we give up.

2. **Obsession gets you to excellence** – with practice and sheer determination the human mind can make the human body overcome all manner of situations.

3. **Gold is won in the mind before it is won in reality** – Bethany should act as a reminder to us all that we need to commit to our goals and believe that we can succeed with 100% confidence.

Quick Summary

- Micro-expressions are quick and fleeting, and leak when we attempt to conceal our true emotional reaction. By improving our ability to read people, we can increase collaboration in our interpersonal relationships and establish a greater rapport with people.

- Power posing, even for two minutes, has a direct impact on our mental and biological processes, which in turn influence our behaviour and, therefore, how we are perceived by others.

- It can be beneficial to engage in deeper relationships and understand more about ourselves by expanding the arena through a process of self-discovery, feedback from others and disclosure to others.

Activity

Watch Amy Cuddy's TED Talk on non-verbal commutation and then try power posing for two minutes before creating an opportunity to negotiate. This could be a free coffee, a discount on your home phone bill or just some good old-fashioned bartering for a discount on the next big-ticket item that you purchase. Notice and write down the differences in the way that you feel and the way you hold yourself in the interaction. What did you notice? How did you feel during the negotiation? What was the result? Did the negotiation create any indirect benefits?

6

THE POWER OF SILENCE

'Nothing strengthens authority as much as silence'
Leonardo Da Vinci

IN THIS CHAPTER, I will show you how to use silence as your secret weapon to control the pace of the negotiation and highlight where rookie mistakes are made. Wielding the power of silence to your advantage takes practice, discipline and skill but will transform your negotiation abilities from basic to advanced.

6.1 Listening and Silence

A question I get asked a lot is, how can I get better at negotiations in business? What can I do? The answer is simple – listen.

We often assume too much. We assume that we know what others want, what price they will pay and what the driving motivators for their business are. The reality is, unless we stop and ask and then truly listen, we are setting ourselves up to fail from the start. However, knowing when to stay silent is right up there as one of the biggest negotiation tools. The reason I say this is many people know that listening is an integral part of negotiating; however, it's the power of silence that seals the deal. In this chapter, I will show you how to utilise a combination of listening and staying silent to become a master negotiator.

Effective listening is a popular topic that is frequently covered in leadership coaching, MBAs and self-development courses. Many negotiation and coaching experts will tell you that effective listening is important when negotiating and they'd be right. There certainly is much to gain from picking up on the cues and specific details that are leaked when your counterpart is talking. I'd even go as far as to say that the more you can get the other person to talk, the more you are likely to hear about their motivations and what they need from the deal. This is beneficial as it could be used to keep the negotiation moving forward. Silence and how to use it to your advantage is a different skill entirely. Although it involves listening, its main focus is control. It is like a secondary sense. The other benefit of silence is it allows you to control the pace of the conversation. By using this intuitive tool, you can resist the urge to respond automatically, which is especially important in a heated or emotionally charged negotiation.

What I want you to understand is that we must know when to stay silent. This skill is used in combination with listening. By knowing the opportune moment to stay silent, a powerful force is unleashed that will have a big impact. If you're able to control that force and feel comfortable with the silence, then it's likely that the other party will fill the void. By default, this means they will continue talking. Not only does this give you more time to think, prepare your answers and take in what the other person is saying, it also provides the opportunity for control. A large part of negotiating is controlling our emotional state. Sometimes things are said in negotiations and the pressure builds; it's easy to snap back with an answer that we later regret.

If negotiators aren't aware of the power of silence, they will have a propensity to jump the gun. With all the excitement and fun of the negotiation, these poor fellows generally get caught up in a cycle that sees their negotiation unravel in a matter of seconds.

The reason why I suggest you focus on using your silence as a tool, is that people who are being coached to listen have a tendency to go: 'Okay, that's fine. I'll listen really hard, until it's my time to speak.'

Or even worse, after they've made their request, they then justify it and fill in the gaps by continually speaking. For example, they make an appropriate and confident request, such as, 'Can I get a discount?' or 'What deal can we do?' Then, all of a sudden, the urge to speak rises up inside them, and like a moth to a flame, they jump back into the conversation and keep on speaking.

It goes something like this…

Request: 'Is there any wiggle room on price?'

One second, two second, ah, there it is… the impulse to fill the void.

Justification: 'I've just spent a lot of money on a new garage, and now things are a bit tight.'

This is exactly where they lose the deal, right there, gone! Right when the other party is mulling it over and debating in their mind the deal is possible, they jump in and start *justifying* why they're asking for it, instead of staying SILENT. By offering more information, you rob the request of its power and provide the other party with the opportunity to stop their thinking in its tracks and refocus on what you have just said.

In this example, your justification for asking for a deal is that you have overspent on another purchase and so times are tough. An astute negotiator could look at this as both a gross mismanagement of funds and an over-indulgence on your part. They may then draw parallels with their own business and its financial health, making the argument that they too have bills to pay.

In actual fact, you could be handing them the golden ticket not to give you a deal by inadvertently directing their attention towards their own financial situation, rather than considering the options available to them for striking a deal.

The other thing justification does is it puts you on the back foot. The very fact that you justify your request can in some cases look desperate, like there was no other reason for doing you a deal that would be a positive idea.

Justification can be used in a positive manner if it causes you to bond with the other person, and they relate to your situation. However, that's a big 'if'. It's not that justification in itself is a rookie error; it's the nature of it, and the reason why you are doing it. In other words, you are justifying your request because you believe this is needed to secure the deal, rather than because you believe the other party has experienced the same thing, and by revealing these details you will open up an opportunity for mutual relatability. The difference is control; in the first scenario it's fear-based, 'The deal won't happen unless I tell them I really need it', rather than, 'I believe this person can relate to me and we can, therefore, have more in common. So it's not the justification that's the issue; it's the motivation behind the justification, and whether it is your natural style when things get uncomfortable as a result of silence.

By becoming an expert in knowing when to stay silent, you will not only benefit from the revelation of new data points by the other person speaking, but also maintain an equal balance of power in the negotiation.

6.2 Filling the Gap

In contrast, negotiators who do not have the discipline of silence firmly planted in their mind will often weaken their position in several ways. The most common way is responding too quickly with 'filler' words that imply their understanding and signal an agreement to the requests.

For example:

Negotiator 1: 'Is there any wiggle room on price?'
Impulse to fill the void

Negotiator 1: 'I've just spent a lot of money on a new garage, and now things are a bit tight.'

Negotiator 2: 'The best I can do is $10,000.'

Negotiator 1: 'Yep' or 'Okay, got it' or 'Um' or 'I hear you.'

When tiny phrases such as these slip out, they automatically chip away at the structure of your negotiation and put you in an unnecessarily difficult position. It's like you have already agreed to their suggestion before you've actually had time to process it.

Over time these little slips will build up and generate the overall signal that you're actually happy with the direction in which the negotiation is going.

Imagine you're Leonardo Di Vinci creating a sculpture and every time you let one of these unnecessary 'filler' phrases slip out it's like taking a chunk out of the masterpiece. Eventually, the sculpture is nothing like you wanted and it's your job to keep it intact.

The sculpture in this example represents your needs and what you want out of in the negotiation. If you imagine that every time you speak you will be taking the chisel to the masterpiece, you'll want to be sure that you are aiming in the right place. Everything you say, even little micro-expressions, are important.

It's your responsibility to get comfortable with silence and the way to do this is to breathe. After you or your counterpart have made a request, just hold it in, instead of nodding or letting out a 'yep', 'OK', or any kind of acknowledgement slip out. Keep the silence, and whatever you do, don't agree. My number one tip is to breathe in, because by doing this, you are giving the impression that you're taking in the new information and thinking it over, and by doing this you're retaining your value in the negotiation.

Another tip is to imagine beforehand what they might request so that you have at least envisaged this moment. Practice in your mind receiving the information without agreeing to it verbally or with a micro-expression, and then just hold the silence.

6.3 Silence and Teams/Pairs

The other issue with silence comes when we negotiate in pairs; now, this can be tricky. Let's say you understand how powerful silence can be. You want to operate in this way in your negotiations, but there's one problem; your partner is all in. They don't have time for silence; they just want to get the deal done. Hell, they are not even aware that silence is a strategic play and you are exhibiting exceptional levels of self-control being able to pull this off. They just think you're being quiet.

There have been multiple situations when I've quite happily held my silence, feeling comfortable with the negotiation. However, my colleague has looked over and felt the need to fill the uncomfortable void. Not only is this frustrating as hell, it's very hard to explain to them after the negotiation has finished that this method was designed to keep the other side talking.

My top tip is get your partner onside beforehand. If they don't know what you are up to, then explain it to them because you need to be on the same page before going into the negotiation, and that means knowing who will take the lead, as well as what the strategy around silence will be.

And even then, there can still be deviations from the course when they start speaking. Be prepared for this and try not to get frustrated when it happens. Negotiating in pairs is either the best thing ever or can be incredibly difficult.

Dealing with the discomfort of silence, making a request or being asked a direct question is tough. It takes practice, just as knowing exactly when to speak does.

Developing a working relationship with your negotiation partner takes time, experience and persistence. Over time, you and your partner will learn to read each other. You will develop an innate intuition or instinct that will kick when you are actually in need of support and you can reap the rewards of silence, Anyone's mind can go blank at any time, so having a partner who recognises the signs and can jump in before the other party realises it is vital and will provide solid teamwork.

Negotiating in pairs often happens in business. The trouble is you will need to become very good at it together. You will need to know how the other person operates and feel comfortable that they know where they are going with the negotiation. There's nothing worse than knowing that you are playing the game, controlling your emotions and developing your skill, but your partner takes your silence as a sign of panic, and then proceeds to answer the question, responding as best they can.

Not only does this feel crappy, it discredits the whole process and makes it look you didn't know what to do and were being silent because you were stuck. It's a tricky one, which is why it's so important to get obsessed about knowing each other to the Nth degree. That way your partner will be able to relax when there is a moment of silence. Knowing each other is a key factor in successful negotiation. Being able to build each other up and bounce off each other is as important as what you say. Knowing when to be vocal and when to remain silent is undoubtedly the most important aspect of that equation, as it allows you to wield control of the negotiation.

You know what they say: 'People won't remember what you said, but they will remember how you made them feel.' So when working in a pair, the other party will pick up on how well you know each other and work together. In situations when this goes well, you will be unstoppable.

Behaving in a certain way, playing silent and answering when ready, will not automatically guarantee you success unless it's authentic. Rather than this being a strategy for negotiation, it should be the negotiation; the way that you interact and influence the path that the negotiating takes.

This way, there is no façade; it's real, it's what you intended to happen. You haven't got imposter syndrome; it's authentic and it is felt in the moment. You must know each other well because moments of gold created by a strategically intended pause can so easily be ruined through a misunderstanding between partners. This will leave value on the table and make it difficult to ever regain that same level of presence in the negotiation.

It's like revealing your cards and then asking for advice. It changes the way the negotiation is perceived. Silence is golden but it also must be handled with care, like a tiger in a zoo. It looks pretty and it is effective, but it can still leave you with a nasty scratch.

The best way to overcome this if you are negotiating with a new partner is to decide upfront who's taking the lead. That way it is clear who is driving and executing this negotiation forward.

As you build up your experience of negotiating together and get a range of rich experiences together, you will begin to bounce off each other.

By practising together on a series of low value negotiations you can build up a bank of experiences and start to understand each other's styles and strengths. There will be certain parts of the negotiation that you each individually excel at.

One of you may be good at the small talk before the negotiation begins, putting the other party at ease. The other may be good at asking direct questions that get results and reveals key information that drives the negotiation forward. You may be skilled at setting the scene and reading the room, picking up key details from a long time ago and recalling them. Whatever they are, you will each have your strengths and you will find that in every negotiation, some of them will be more important than others.

The key to successful negotiation is to recognise what is most important and needed at the specific time and then play that card. When you are both in sync, you will experience flow. The negotiation will seem effortless and you will instinctively know who is leading at which part as you move forward.

The other part of negotiating in pairs is making sure that you have all the information. It's highly damaging to start down the path in a negotiation without having all the same facts, as you will end up in a scenario where your partner has to correct you on details surrounding the deal. These will have already been negotiated, agreed upon, discussed, or are out of date due to changes in the market (such as an acquisition) that have made what you are saying irrelevant.

This will damage your credibility and is it hard to recover from this. So it's best practice to have a pre-negotiation catch-up with your partner beforehand to make sure that you are aware of all the facts and can play to your best. Not allowing time for this step, or walking into the room without even so much as a quick five-minute conversation with you partner, is negligent and leaves you open to exploitation.

The key problem here is, if the other party cottons on to the fact that you haven't had a chance to go over key details of the negotiation or exchanged deal sensitive information with your partner prior to stepping into the room, they may very well use this to their advantage.

This can easily be done by getting you to reveal more key details or overshare potentially sensitive information, unaware of how this leaves you exposed. Alternatively, they might call your bluff, already knowing that if you respond incorrectly then you are bluffing. By doing this, they will want to see: a) if you are going to try to bluff them as part of your style, which will give them information on how you like to operate and indicate to them that you may do so again in the future; or b) if your partner jumps in to save you from making the blunder.

For example, it will make a mockery of the process if you walk into a negotiation without knowing that your partner has already set the benchmarks for price at $2,000 based on a deal they openly stated they did last week, and you explain that it is not in the company's interests to do a deal for less than $5,000, and this has never been offered before.

A savvy negotiator will see through this and call you on it. As a result, your credibility and confident presentation of the information will be challenged. It doesn't matter whether it was a miscommunication of information or a mistake, the core problem is that you look uninformed and someone who is spouting company lines, rather than offering them true value. In essence, your authenticity will become compromised, not to mention the professionalism of how you both operate together in business.

My top tips for negotiating in pairs are:

1. Treat each other as the same mind; always think from the other's perspective and be aware of what your partner doesn't know.
2. Have a pre-negotiation sync; make it a habit to go over key details and exchange information, strategy and outcome preferences.
3. Be in constant communication with each other. If the information has changed, how will you let your partner know about it? It's not always possible to meet in person, so you need to establish how you can keep each other in the loop before walking into that room and beginning the negotiation.
4. It's better to reschedule the negotiation than to wing it.
5. If in doubt, and you think some of the details may have already been covered, don't be afraid to ask and let your partner provide a summary of what has happened during the meeting. This is an excellent way of getting up to speed while responding appropriately to the other party.

It's a beautiful thing when you can learn to negotiate in a pair, but it takes repeated practice, consistent communication and concentration. Each person must always be thinking from the perspective of the other.

There is an endless list of reasons why the other party will play on any gaps in knowledge during the negotiation. They will try and draw out information, discredit you or just play the game but, ultimately, it comes down to dividing the group.

If there's an opportunity where they can either discredit you by showing that you don't have all the facts or proving outright that you are bluffing, they will take it as this will leave you isolated from the negotiation going forward. It will weaken your position, as well as the level of influence you have going forward.

In short, some negotiators will use this as their tactic to divide the group early on, as it means that instead of having two people to deal with, they will now only have one.

It's also embarrassing because these are long-term relationships and it will be hard to move past this impression and establish authority in the relationship when you deal with this party again in the future. Psychologically, it places you at a disadvantage in the relationship. Think of it like walking into an interview without knowing what the company does. As soon as the interviewer realises you are blind to some of the facts, it's difficult to recover from; not just in that moment, but in the future as well.

So ensure that you and your partner prepare in the same way you would for an important interview by thinking of the questions that might be asked, especially about the relationship and the details of the deal. What the other party is looking for here are differences or cracks in the response. If they find any, then they'll keep pushing to see if the cracks open up. The way to counter this is to have both the same story and same facts, and to enjoy the process together. You must be watertight as a pair.

There's no better feeling in negotiation than knowing that you are up to date. You have all the facts of the matter, you know where the boundaries are, you have the autonomy to free flow in the negotiation, and your partner is experienced in the way you move.

Quick Summary

- Silence is a way to gain control that requires discipline, but once it's mastered, it can be used to control the pace of the negotiation, which is an important dynamic.
- Negotiating in pairs increases the complexity and risks of using silence as a as a tool. If it's done correctly and in the appropriate context, both negotiators in the negotiating pair will be on the same page and it will be the ultimate force.
- Resist the urge to 'fill the gap' or justify yourself after making your request.

Activity

Over the next 24 hours, I challenge you to watch your automatic reactions and responses and take note of them. These say more about you than they do the other person. If you find you have a tendency to fill the void, justify, respond or agree with the other person hastily, then note it down as this is the first stage to building up your negotiation muscle. If this is you, then fear not. All this is telling us is that we have more work to do. It's a signal that you don't fully, 100% believe that it is possible.

Bonus activity for improving negotiation in pairs

1. Get to know your negotiation partner inside and out; find out what their strengths are.
2. Where do you have strengths duplication?

3. What do you excel at in negotiation? Spend some time thinking about how you will operate. By getting into the habit of chatting regularly before the negotiations, you set the expectation that this is how you will operate moving forward. This is a world-class habit to get into.

4. It's also vitally important to debrief afterwards and to share what you have each noticed. It could be in the cab on the way back to the office. Make sure it's directly after the negotiation if possible, as this increases the likelihood that you won't miss or forget any key details. Use this time to brainstorm ideas as to how you will move forward. It is also a great time to celebrate the wins and share in that bonding experience. My advice is that you should not miss this stage, celebrate the small wins, embrace how well you worked together, and have fun with the result. This is where the magic happens that sets you up for success next time and reinforces what you both did well, so that you will remember to do it again next time.

On the journey to mastery, think of this as the gym. It is where you can build up muscle, gain self-efficacy and expand the foundation on which you have to play. As you move forward working as a pair, you'll start to expand this pattern and it will happen naturally. It doesn't have to be formal; that's not the point. The point is that it happens. Like any professional team, you are two people that start together and end together. That's the real beauty of a negotiation team and that's where the fun is. Being able to go out and regroup and share in the successes and the losses; that's how successful negotiators operate. It's how they get to know each other and become better at working together.

PART 4

BE A SUCCESSFUL NEGOTIATOR

7

STRATEGIES AND TACTICS FOR SUCCESSFUL NEGOTIATION

'Strategy without tactics is the slowest route to victory.
Tactics without strategy is the noise before defeat.'

Sun Tzu

7.1 Negotiate the Negotiation

IN THIS CHAPTER, I aim to pull it all together by giving you a range strategies and tactics for successful negotiation that you will be able to apply in a range of contexts. Having a strategy, and knowing which one is appropriate and in which context, comes with experience. As I shared with you at the beginning of the book, I have built up my skill over time through experience. We are not born with the gift of being a top negotiator. I have made many, many mistakes and it's through those times of repeated failure that I have learned more about myself and other people in the process. What I am to give you here is a selection of only a few strategies and tactics that you can use to approach the negotiation table in a successful way. Remember that strategy is also what we uncover and decide to do in the negotiation preparation phase. Michael Porter defines strategy as 'choosing what not to do', which comes from careful consideration of all the elements at play. Having an excellent strategy and engaging one or a few tactics to expedite that strategy is like going from being the occasional chess player to becoming a chess master. It takes time, consideration and experience to know what not to do and the best way to execute a strategy in anticipation of who you are dealing with and the factors involved. My hope is that by this point you will understand how to analyse the information that you already know about the upcoming negotiation and can formulate a strategy that will maximises the outcomes.

It took two years to write this book. I crafted it, piece by piece. I wrote it out once and sent it off for review by a trusted manuscript agency; their feedback was firm but fair. Based on this, I then promptly rewrote it over the course of three months. However, what you are reading now is probably version number 84. Like negotiation, it takes time to write, edit and perfect. I wanted to inject a sense of anything is possible into the book. So, I started reaching out to people who I admired to see if they wanted to answer a few questions on negotiation. One of the best books I have ever read is *Give and Take* by Adam Grant. When I read this book it quickly became the most annotated book in my collection; there was so much value. I promoted it to all my friends and sent them copies at Christmas. It changed my thinking and I am confident it will also give you value. Adam is an Organisational Psychologist, Wharton Professor and a *New York Times* bestselling author.

Case study: Adam Grant's take on Negotiation

I decided to reach out to Adam to see if he'd like to share his thoughts on negotiation for this book. I was in luck; he came back to me within a couple of days and answered the following question that I posed to him.

Question: In a world where hardball negotiators are glamourised by the media and environments, where power and dominance are celebrated, how do we have a more open conversation and disarm to achieve more successful negotiations?

Adam's response was thoughtful and deeply interesting, I knew his take on this question would be world class. Here's what he said:

> When I worked as a negotiator, I found that having a meta-conversation made a big difference. Before negotiating, I would negotiate about how we were going to negotiate. So there are two ways we can handle this negotiation. One is to have a friendly conversation about what we're both trying to accomplish and see if we can help each other. I prefer to do it that way. The other option is to play hardball, where we try to take advantage of each other. I don't enjoy it, but if that's how you want to do it.

So, let's break down what Adam's saying here. He's giving the other person two options when it comes to the way that the negotiation can take place by stating upfront, hey buddy, there are two roads we can take to get this deal done – which one do you want to travel? It's a clever strategy because it calls out the fact that the opportunity to take advantage of each other is there, but it's not a road he'd prefer to go down. Through this strategy, it's easy to see how the subsequent negotiations after this meta-conversation were likely to go down the friendly route more often than not. By stating what's there, this strategy of negotiating how the negotiation is going to take place calls for a commitment upfront to the process and takes the heat out of it.

Adam continues...

7.2 Trust

Another strategy is trust and recognising that if you want to be trusted, you have to start by showing it yourself. You can do that by selectively sharing information and revealing one of your interests that doesn't put you in a compromising position. If the person reciprocates, you can open up a little more in the next round.

Adam's advice is spot on: the best way to build trust is to show trust and lead by example. Trust can be a pre-condition of negotiation in certain contexts and cultures; the Chinese, for example, invest heavily in cultivating trust prior to their business engagements.

It can also be used as a strategy for integrative negotiation; for example, there are mutual benefits to working collaboratively to expand the scope of the original negotiation and working towards a longer-term exchange of reward. The downside of trust as a strategy is that it may inhibit you from seeking a competitive advantage in your negotiations in favour of the long-term relationship; this is true, even if the benefits outweigh the cost. In win-win negotiation strategy, where the relationship is built on trust, it could damage the future of the relationship if one party decided to act on a competitive advantage. It could resemble a strategic shift in the power dynamic and, thus, cause the end of the mutually beneficial exchange.

The other way in which trust appears in negotiations is as an objective or goal of the negotiation itself. There are many facets to negotiation and gaining the trust of one party could be considered to be a strategic advantage and, therefore, directly pursued as an outcome of the negotiation. For example, if a smaller country wanted to negotiate with a larger, powerful country and their objective was to use the negotiation as a method of building trust with that country to form a strategic alliance.

And if that wasn't enough, Adam provides a third example of how to have more open negotiations.

7.3 Humour (Pet Frog)

And a third option is to add some humour to lighten the mood and create a human connection. There's a classic negotiation experiment showing that you're more likely to reach a deal if you say, 'I'll throw in my pet frog.'

In the study, Adam is referring to researchers Karen O'Quin and Joel Aronoff (1981) who explored the effect of humour in a bargaining situation. They conducted an experiment whereby participants were asked to buy a painting and instructed to negotiate the sale price with a seller (the seller was in on the study). In one variation of the study, the seller responded with a humorous offer, 'Well, my final offer is $100 and I'll throw in my pet frog,' while in the other variation no humour was used. The results of the study tell us a story – those in the humorous condition agreed to pay an average higher price than those in the non-humorous condition. If you weren't sold on humour already, you need to be; humour provides a huge advantage in sales negotiations.

But what's really going on here? Is humour just a tool to get people to like you more?

Well, I'm glad you asked; these researchers didn't stop there either. They took the explanation of the results one step further. Through deeper analysis of the findings, they concluded that it wasn't just the humour that caused the buyer to like the seller more and pay the higher sale price, but it did allow the buyer to perceive the seller wasn't taking the negotiation seriously and they could, therefore, 'save face' by agreeing to a higher price. So, in essence, humour is the bridge that allows ego to be put aside because the buyer saw the situation as less threatening. Interestingly, the results also showed that subjects exposed to humour enjoyed the task more, and that shouldn't be ignored. Humour in negotiations can not only ease tension but also transition the bargaining away from the winner takes all strategies to a more malleable playing field.

So there you have it; add a little humour into your negotiations and you might be able to get a higher price for your painting. I'm joking; there is a place and time for humour, and your assessment of the situation and judgement of when to use humour appropriately is key. However, generally speaking, a little humour and a pet frog can go a long way.

7.4 Upfront Full Disclosure

Another strategy is to be upfront and honest about your goal at the beginning of the negotiation. By revealing your intention, you are actually setting expectations that you want a deal. 'We're going to do a deal, I'm looking for a discount, at least 25 points off. I know we can make it happen so I may as well put it out there.' This is a bold strategy but by doing this you are indicating that you intend to get a better deal and are giving specific reference to the level of discount that you want. Remember, this concept can be applied to anything, not just discounts. I am just using that as an example. Once stated there is a small window of opportunity for the seller to respond, but if it is missed then the negotiation will proceed with this statement still hanging in the air. It flags to the seller that this is where you're headed and psychologically there's a shift in understanding. By making this intention clear from the start, there can be no misunderstanding that a discount is required to make a sale.

If the seller doesn't respond with a rebuttal then, it's now your job to bring this to a close and execute on your intention for a discount. Say something like, 'So you know I want a deal, what level of discount can you apply. Can you reach our 25%?'

This brings the very real intention to the fore and reframes it as a question. It's then up to the seller to come to the table. The benefit of this strategy is that it's bold; there are no surprises. This means that any relationship that's formed between the start and the end of the negotiation can exist, fully independent of the request. Boldness speaks to authenticity; in some cases it can be just what's needed to get the deal done.

The potential downside of this strategy (depending on how you look at it) is it can bring the negotiation to a close pretty quickly, unless you decide to continue it anyway. If no perceived opportunity for a deal is uncovered upfront and the seller responds with 'we don't do discounts', then it makes it clear that more work will be required at the close of the negotiation. It also provides a reference point for the seller when you request a discount at a later stage, as they can say: 'Like I said, we don't do discounts.' The strategy here must be to focus on the exception to the rule.

I once walked into Billabong store, as I was in the market for a new wetsuit. If you've ever been wetsuit shopping you'll know that they are damn expensive, but you get into it pretty fast, and before you know it, the only thing you want between you and the ocean is a top of the range piece of kit that hugs the contours of your body like an obsessed lover. So there I was, faced with a large expense. I walked in and boldly asked the first sales guy I saw, 'I need a wetsuit, they're very expensive, can you do a discount.' To my surprise the guy turned to me and said, 'Well, it's my last day, I will give you my staff discount of 40%.' I was over the moon, we went to the rack and picked off the best wetsuit I'd seen in my life; it was a good day. Now I know what some of you sceptics might be thinking. It was only because he was a nice guy and it was his last day that he gave you a discount, and in a logical sense you'd be right, but the point is it was the act of asking upfront for a discount that got the deal. Just think, there are plenty of opportunities that go unrealised every day because people don't ask upfront. By closing the deal from the start, you are actually creating the deal in some cases.

7.5 Honesty

Always, always choose the information that you would like to share; don't be dishonest. There's no need to lie during a negotiation and once you do, it's like getting married; you're wedded to that lie.

Your story will unravel and you will look less credible as a result. When the other party starts to doubt your story, they will start to doubt you, and so your credibility will go out the window, and so too will the deal. Lies and negotiation don't mix.

The best way to handle a tricky or potentially tough negotiation is to remember you have a choice; a choice about how and when you reveal the information that you want to share. You shouldn't need to lie to make the wheels turn. It's not that it won't work; it may do, but the long-term standing of your relationship will forever be damaged. It's better to be upfront and clear about what you need from the deal.

The other part about lying is the emotional baggage that comes with it. The negotiation won't feel like a real win (because you haven't used your best practice skills to get there) and it will hang over you like a grey cloud.

What feels good to us humans is real success that comes as a result of experience, skill and action. When lies get added to the equation it becomes more difficult to control the negotiation because, ultimately, there are now more variables involved. There's you, them, the specifics of the deal and your little friend, the lie. This gets further intensified with the introduction of more people into the equation, so it acts like a multiplier.

You + Them + Specifics + (LIE) x number of people = Chaos + emotional baggage

New people joining the negotiation will perhaps not know about the lie and, therefore, your stress will increase as a result. This will lead you to leaking more signs of anxiety, not because of the pressure the other person is putting you under, but as a result of the lie. But the other person will not perceive it like this, as they don't know you've lied. They'll see you sweating and think it's down to them. They'll think that your uncomfortable because of elements of the deal. In some situations, this could then be used against you, which is less than ideal. In the worst-case scenario, you will be exposed to, or agree to, a less preferable deal just to end the negotiation (exiting early).

Another element of this is being honest with ourselves, which comes back to engaging with the right questions. How badly do I need this deal to go through? How much do I have on the line if it doesn't? Honesty is a two-way street with yourself, so understand your boundaries.

7.6 Keep It Simple

Leonardo Da Vinci once said, 'Simplicity is the ultimate sophistication,' and he was right. When we are honest, we have direction and the pathway to follow is clear. This is an important skill that's paramount in successful negotiation. Simplicity is key. Why? Because it helps you to articulate in the negotiation; if a deal is too complex or can't be simply explained, then it is likely to fall over for all manner of reasons. The biggest of which is, 'I don't understand it; therefore, I can't proceed'. Ego gets in the way here, and sometimes people do not say outright what the reason is because they don't understand. They'll just say that we can't do the deal and make up a reason. But behind it, sitting there, is the fact they just don't understand it and, therefore, they can't trust it.

The other great part about understanding something and being able to explain a deal in a simple and easy way to follow, is that it makes you look awesome!

People love to feel like they understand something that's complex; it makes them feel important and useful.

7.7 Best Alternative to a Negotiated Agreement (BATNA)

The term was first coined by Roger Fisher and William Ury in their 1981 book on negotiation, called *Getting to Yes: Negotiating without giving in*.

This is not to be confused with the 'bottom line'. The BATNA represents an alternative option outside of the negotiation, which will be opted for if an agreement cannot be reached in an appropriate time frame.

Having a strong BATNA represents a source of power (a topic that we'll cover a little later on) to enhance the strength of your BATNA. Before going into the negotiation, one should brainstorm all of the alternative options available to the individual and then proceed to make them a reality so that they can become viable.

For example, a BATNA could be going into a pay rise negotiation with an attractive alternative job offer in hand that is ready to be accepted should your negotiation go south. It acts as a plan B in the event that an agreement can't be reached.

As world-class negotiators, we should be on the lookout for, and be directly involved in, the process of creating BATNA as a backup plan to our negotiations. This should form part of the pre-negotiation planning phase. Remember, the other side may also engage in developing their BATNA, and if you are either unprepared for this or fail to explore your own BATNA, then you may be subject to huge internal pressure to reach an agreement.

In the event that both parties have strong BATNAs, then it may not always be advantageous for the parties to reach an agreement and, therefore, opt in favour of the BATNAs. Because if each party's BATNA is suitably desirable, then there will be little or no incentive to stick to the original negotiation process of bargaining for agreement.

In the event that you are offered terms that are below your BATNA, you should walk away from the negotiation and choose to opt for your BATNA instead. In reality, your BATNA is rarely going to be like comparing 'apples to apples'. For example, you might be negotiating for a lamp at a market. You know there is an alternative lamp (your BATNA) for sale at $50 on another stall; therefore, if you can't get the desired lamp for $50, you opt for the BATNA. Or in another scenario, you might be comparing the annual renewal of your gym membership, credit cards or car insurance to your current provider. By going into the negotiation armed with the facts about other policies, you may have another option should a relevant BATNA be identified.

As mentioned before, your BATNA is not your bottom line. Your bottom line is the final barrier where the negotiation will not proceed any further if it is crossed; it's the worst terms you'll accept in a deal before walking away.

7.8 Create a Sense of Urgency

A top negotiator knows when to create a sense of urgency. It takes a combination of courage and skill to leverage this tactic. By doing this, you are ultimately aiming to close the negotiation. However, you don't need to use this tactic only in the closing phase. The skill is knowing what the negotiation needs. If it requires pushing along, then a healthy sense of competition early on will create the necessary momentum. Or if a more tactile approach is needed, then only reveal the need for action at the final stages.

Realtors do this all the time; for example, by coordinating property showings so that one viewing coincides with another potential buyer leaving the building. This creates an environment of increased demand and plants the seeds of desire. In Australia, all property viewings are conducted at the same time in a window of just 15 minutes. This is strategic, to cause potential tenants to act on emotion, drive up bids and act on impulses governed by the fear of missing out. You can leverage these tactics for your own business or your own needs by displaying an active market to the other side. Whether it is staged or real, you will tap into human emotions.

For example, your work colleague could call you when you are with a potential client to say you are low on stock. This creates the need to make a decision if they want to get in on the action.

Another way would be to pull the deal, or alluding to the fact that the deal will be off the table due to other interested parties having made an offer. For example, you may find that if you reject a second-round job interview on the grounds of low remuneration (which was discussed when you conducted your first sense checking) the company will review both the offer and the role to get you back into the process. Or, if you have made it through to the final round but haven't heard from them for a few days (3 or more) when they said they would ring, it's absolutely OK to give them a call. State that you have had other offers which you need to make a decision on, so you need to know where you stand. It might sound odd to reject something that you want, but it's like dating, people want what they can't have. By creating the impression that you may be going elsewhere, it will cause the company to make a decision. This is a great position to be in because they will chase you if they want you. Whereas when you are waiting and waiting for them to come back to you, they are busy interviewing other candidates, making it less likely that they will offer you the position, which damages your chances and negotiating power. By taking yourself off the table, the company is almost compelled to want you more due to the fact that they can't have you.

Other ways of creating a sense of urgency:

- Specials
- One time deals – take it or leave it

- Low on stock
- Other offers
- Competition offers, price, quotes, time
- Retracting the offer

To create a sense of urgency, you need to think outside the box and get creative. You can have a friend run into you and say they have heard so and so wants to buy your car when you are showing it to another potential buyer. Then, quickly summarise the benefits and push hard to close deal. It's a one, two, approach, event + benefits + request (e.g. do you want to take the car?) = deal closed. It should hit the other side as if by magic, at speed. First, they see that the deal is potentially vanishing in front of their eyes and then you are presenting them with an ultimatum and a possible route to secure the deal. They should first feel what it is like not to have the deal, and then, bam, you resurrect it with one caveat – they need to act now.

When you create a sense of urgency you need to hold firm. If the other side tries to negotiate, hold steady. Do not entertain their offer unless it's a remarkably favourable deal that makes sound business sense. If, however, it's just their first offer, do not entertain it, as it will make a mockery of your negotiation process and make them understand they have all the power in the negotiation. Instead, you should hold firm, create the urgency, e.g. say that you're not sure you even want to sell the car anymore. Tell them point blank that you can't sell it for that price. It will go round and round and ultimately, if you hold firm and state the price for sale, and get them to state the price they are willing to pay, they'll come up and meet your needs or get pretty damn close. Once you state a lower price, you'll be on a landslide. So only state the lower price when it's the one that you are willing to accept, and you are ready to close the deal. This might sound harsh, but unless you are willing to hold firm and stand your ground, you'll have trouble getting the value you deserve. By creating an active market, you give yourself more options and comparison points. It's a clever way of ensuring both a BATNA and some healthy competition at the same time.

7.9 Red Flags and Warning Signs

Talking of walking away; when should we negotiate? Or to rephrase the question, when is negotiation not appropriate?

Like with anything else, there are always a few unforeseen, non-negotiable situations. Then there are those that you're better off avoiding all together and rescheduling until a more appropriate time.

In this chapter, we've focused on strategies, like trust building, humour and emotions, that can achieve successful outcomes, but now let's take a look at the red flags when it comes to negotiating and how you can approach a potentially volatile situation and still get the outcome that you want.

Remember the goal of successful negotiation is win-win, but that doesn't mean it has to be instant. Negotiations require time and patience, so knowing when and how to approach them is key to understanding why negotiations can still be successful under stressful conditions.

People can often go into a negotiation viewing the other person as an enemy they must defeat, but viewing negotiation from this perspective is a mistake. Negotiation is an art, and like all art forms, some people are naturally more talented from the start, but the skills and techniques can be taught, honed and improved upon so that you can become a master. If you want to learn and pay attention to the subtleties of human behavior, you can refine your techniques and leverage all your experiences to become a natural.

There are some cases where it is best to walk away from a negotiation. For example, if anger is involved, it's best practice to revisit the negotiation at a later stage when the anger has subsided, rather than aggravate the other party and damage the relationship.

Another example is when the other party is 'showing off', and are willing to sabotage the negotiation just to prove a point. It is often better to move on and find another deal. In the case of a cocky show off, their ego is out to party and they will go out of their way to induce a stalemate situation or, even worse, lose money just to prove a point.

Rather than try to rationalise and work with this type of behaviour, it's better to put it in the 'you can't lose something that was never there box' and walk away. If the other party will not negotiate in a mutually respectful fashion, even if it is detrimental to their business and future relationships, then cut your losses; this is a not a successful negotiation that you want to be involved with.

My philosophy is you should always be prepared for a negotiation, unless you're dealing with an unhinged party or an unrealistic showoff. My advice is to be 'always on' and try to spot opportunities for negotiation first (by the end of this book it should be automatic). See the opportunity, then decide if it is appropriate to take it or not. This process trains your mind to be on the lookout, so that you are ready to take on a negotiation if it comes your way or create an opportunity if you see fit. As we've discussed, negotiations happen everywhere. Don't be put off by stress or feeling awkward; instead, seek to find maximum value for both parties. If you believe this is the optimum time, then go for it with no holds barred. If you find out that it's not what you thought and there could be a better time due to an angry recipient or blatant show off, then trust yourself to make that judgement and come back later.

Changing our mindset on negotiation, from one of competition to a valued relationship, is a bit like walking into a new job wanting to impress your new boss. When you arrive at your new job you want to make a good first impression; to be a success and demonstrate your value. The best advice I received about this was to ask yourself: 'What's their biggest pain point?' If you can work that out and actively seek a solution, you'll add value. It's a similar scenario in a negotiation; find out what their pain points are, empathise and show how you can help. This way you will transition from perceived competition to valued relationship because you are, in fact, trying to add value from the beginning.

Knowing when to negotiate is a core skill, and as long as you are practising the process of recognising potentially useful information, you'll start to create a memory bank of triggers and phrases that will signal to you when there may be a negotiation opportunity on the horizon.

7.10 Time it Right

If I have to get a series of negotiations done in a day, I start off with an easy one, to warm up and stretch the muscles. It's all about priority; do the easiest first and then work through them, one after the other in order of priority. When you're on a roll, go for gold and tick off a big one.

Timing is also an important factor to consider. I find the best time to negotiate for me is in the morning when I'm fresh and raring to go. Ultimately, it's based on two variables:

them and you. That's why getting to know your clients well is advantageous; you will know how they like to operate.

7.11: 10 Top Tips for Successful Negotiations

1) **Be humble** – don't go after more than is fair. Relationships matter and people remember what you do to them in business. So don't favour short-term wins and glory in the office to the detriment of your long-term relationships.

2) **Go out of your way to offer a level of service that others don't** – do what you say you are going to do and deliver on your promises. This speaks to accountably and execution.

3) **Don't sweat it** – go out there and give it your best shot, either you learn or you get what you want. At the end of the day, one negotiation or one lesson isn't going to define your career. It's a consistent number of successful negotiations and life experiences that build the foundations and allow you to improve and grow as a negotiator.

4) **Cold call** – the difference between getting a deal over the line and thinking about it is action. Make sure that you are pushing yourself to get out of your comfort zone, out of your own head. Give yourself a goal to cold call seven people in one day. It's a skill that not everyone develops and it will set you apart from the rest. New business development relies on this skill. New partnerships, opportunities to pitch; this is the key to creating your own success.

5) **Avoid the naysayers** – avoid them like the plague. In business, they're everywhere and you will waste valuable time and energy hanging out with them. Surround yourself with those who impress you. You will learn more from them and you will grow. Get

a mentor. This is easier said than done, but if one comes along, ask for help, be flexible and take notes, then emulate them by creating your own version. Hell, cold call someone who impresses you and ask them to be your mentor.

6) **Risk** – taking calculated risks is essential, whether you're young or old. Entrepreneurs do great things because of their ability to manage risk. Negotiators play in the same field; they go out there every day and make it happen.

7) **Imagine where you want to be and then go there** – don't wait to be told what to do; seize the initiative, put in the hard work and deliver the results. Ask for forgiveness later. You'll get noticed.

8) **Prepare** – do whatever it takes to ensure you've got all the information you need; create a scenario plan, conduct 'if then' plans and do some role playing. Don't overprepare, however. Do just enough to make it flow, so you know where you are going.

9) **Don't box yourself in** – just because you do a certain job now, have done certain things and have certain dreams, does not mean this is all you are. Keep an open mind. Believe you can do it.

10) **Don't judge** – people will surprise you. Judgement is a double-edged sword that passes back to you how you treat yourself. Judging others harshly is not good for anybody.

Being able to negotiate is the difference between getting that dream job, that girl, that boy, that internship, that grant, that investment, that life – and not. It is the key to making your life dreams come true.

We must be bold ask the right questions, challenge the status quo and take that step towards the future. Then, we will get that grant or investment, and get it on terms that are sustainable and will build a relationship, rather than only working for the short term and wishing you had asked for a better deal.

Delivering on your promises is the backbone of any successful negotiation. Lying, manipulating or giving unfulfilled promises; these are not you. We are committed to operating with integrity, and doing deals that make sense both on paper and in reality, that can be delivered, sustained and repeated. This is how we will change the world.

I have a question for you: what is the happiest moment of your life?

For me, I've had some of my happiest memories while basking in the ocean in Thailand at sunset, or dancing in London at 3am with my best friends. All the pieces of the jigsaw aligned, they fitted. This is what doing a successful negotiation can feel like. Deep down we all want to feel liberated. So many of us get hooked on travel. We fall in love with the freedom and love the possibility. Please capture this sense of freedom and bring it home with you to your corporate world, to your jobs, your lives and then challenge the status quo.

Negotiation is a melting pot of variables. Remember how you feel when you're enjoying a night out with your best mates? Well, draw that feeling into your negotiations. After all, it should be fun!

Summary

- Having a strong BATNA is a source of power, those with the strongest one tend to do better in negotiations
- By adding humour to your negotiations, you can often extract more value
- Hope is not a strategy. To achieve great things at speed, you must have a clear strategy and the right tactics in place
- Know the warning signs that tell you when you should not proceed in a negotiation, and return to them later

Activity

Now it's time to have some fun and put your skills to the test. I want you to select a negotiation you need to have in your mind. Got one? OK, good. This is your first mini challenge to put your new skills to the test. Write down your clear strategy for the negotiation, including the reasons why you believe this strategy will work and the factors you used to make that decision. Next, pick one of the tactics above and give it a whirl.

For example:

I am going to get a discount on my rent this month. There has been extensive noise created by workers on the roof of the apartment block (legitimacy) and, therefore, I would like compassionate treatment for this inconvenience in the form of me paying less on my monthly rent this month. I choose to use humor as my tactic and believe that calling in the morning is the best time to do so. My strategy is to create a negotiation where a reduction in rent is agreed upon, rather than negotiating whether it is, in fact, possible. To do this, I will begin with clear statements of the objective upfront, e.g. 'Hi Shirley, how are you? I am calling because I would like to get a reduced payment on this month's rent due to the excessive noise created by the worker on the roof. I want to work with you to figure out what an appropriate reduction would look like.' (This will plant the seed of possibility, rather than finding out if it's possible). The conversation could go like this:

'What's your favorite band, Shirley?'

'Queen.'

'Well, it's like we've got Queen playing a full rendition of *Bohemian Rhapsody* up on the roof, it's good for a day but after that it's just painful (humour, ice breaker).'

Pause:

'Not possible, blah, blah, blah.'

'Don't stop me now, Shirley (pun). I would have thought that as we've been respectful and loyal tenants for the past three years, you would at least be able to call the landlord and come up with something that makes sense. Can you please do this for me?' (This moves the request away from negative door closing behaviour and on to actions that create opportunity.)

Have your BATNA ready.

'I don't want to interrupt the landlord.'

'I can appreciate that (showing understanding and agreement). However, this has caused distress for my family and others in the building who I know to have requested a similar agreement. If this can't be resolved between us, then I will need to bring this up with the building manager. Surely there is something you can do to help us? I am happy to have the conversation with the landlord myself or with you, if that helps?' (Creating options against the objections.)

You get the idea. Now it's over to you. Clarify your strategy, goals and tactics upfront and then go out there and give it a red hot go. You will feel liberated and exhilarated by just giving it a shot.

8

21ST CENTURY NEGOTIATIONS

'Our greatest weakness lies in giving up. The most certain
way to succeed is to try just one more time.'

Thomas Edison

NOW THAT YOU'VE got the basic strategies, we can delve
a little deeper... Negotiations can be a bumpy ride so
you need to know what to do when things get tricky. In this
chapter, I will show you how to transition the negotiation
from a dead-end and into an avenue of possibility. We'll take
a look at how to handle asymmetric negotiations when the
other side has more power and what to do to tip the balance
of power back in your direction. We'll also spend some time
looking at techniques, such as anchoring, bargaining and
assumptions, as well as negotiating via social media, and in
case you ever need it, how to deal with hackers. This is the
real meat of the book so pay attention. If you want to be an
expert negotiator you need to be able to weather the storm
by exhibiting resilience and drive when you are faced with a
tricky negotiation.

8.1 How to Turn No Into Yes

Quite simply, the key to this is possibility. Ask yourself this
question: is it possible?

Most things in life are possible, but perhaps they are not so probable. The key to getting a 'No' to turn into a 'Yes, of course, right this way, madam,' is your attitude. You need to be highly driven to be able to create the moment of possibility through what you say, do and how you make the other person feel.

People respond to stimuli. Therefore, you need to present the right stimuli and create the environment in which the key can open the door.

Think of a time when you were told 'no' but you really wanted a 'yes'. Now ask yourself these questions:

- How were you acting in the situation?
- How much rapport did you create?
- Did you smile?
- What vibe were you giving off?
- What mindset did you have going into the situation?
- Was it one of absolute possibility?
- What are you bringing to the situation (e.g. history, biases, subconscious, fear, doubts, expectations?)

As you can see, there are a whole array of factors that contribute to this. What's the one thing more than anything else that gets you from A to B in this context? How do you get the key to turn?

It's charisma; people respond to what they feel. To be a door opener and to possess this key, you need to embrace it.

Think of Leonardo DiCaprio in the film *Catch Me If You Can* (2002). When he became a fake pilot, he owned it! To the outside world, there was no doubting he was a pilot as he marched through Miami airport, with his air hostesses by his side, screaming: 'I am a captain and I am going to fly this plane.' No one challenged him because there was no question or doubts; if anything they were in awe. If others believe it is possible, then all of a sudden it becomes so, but they need to come with you on the journey. They truly need to be with you inside their minds.

The distinction here is you're not begging or trying to pull the wool over anyone's eyes; you're already on the side of possibility and you're asking them to join you there. You need to be bold without trying to be. You need to believe with every fibre of your body that what you are doing, and how you are presenting yourself, is the true you. This can't be an act that you turn on and off; it needs to be authentic. You'll figure out yourself what your style is. Remember, people are more likely to believe what they see if you show them and give them no reason to doubt you. If you achieve this, then you're more than 90% there.

I won't beat around the bush here. In negotiation, you need to be able to turn on your charm. It's not a case of believing it is possible and then making the request. That would be rudimentary and quite frankly fluffy rubbish. The way that you present the information, the picture you paint and how you tell it all makes a difference. Luck plays its part too, but ultimately it comes down to you.

If you are having unsuccessful negotiations and doors just aren't opening, look at what you are bringing to the situation. You need to really analyse objectively how you are being in the interaction, and what biases you are bringing into the situation.

Do you have an ego? Ego is a big one; do you think this door must open because you deserve it? Are you forcing it?

Looking through this introspective lens we must remember that, at its core, this isn't about you; it's about them and how you make them feel. It's a bit like when you fancy someone at a bar and you know it's mutual. You catch each other's eye and it's on; there's a balance between charm, mystery and genuine intrigue. When it's forced, needy and chased, it only puts out the flame. Negotiation is not desperate; it doesn't beg.

What you're looking for is that magic, that spark. When your eyes meet across the bar, you let the night go where it goes. You both engage in the story. You are confident when it is needed, but not ego driven.

One unfortunate consequence that can happen is that people let it go to their head when they start to see results in negotiation and feel themselves excel at it. They then think they deserve a deal, fail to be present in the moment of each negotiation and become careless in their work. They use a string of previous successes as a stick to beat their drum with (e.g. 'I've got this discount before' or 'I've done a deal like this in the past.') This will only get you so far. When you refer to past successes, it is like driving down a short runway; eventually, the runway stops and you end up in the sea. People can feel when you are trying to force something and are desperate; when you need a deal to pump up your ego, rather than for its own sake of being an exceptional deal.

When people allow the deals they make to define them as a person, they start to do bad deals. It becomes more about chasing a deal, as this is where they get their confidence from, rather than having an innate confidence in themselves. The confidence, the 'you' part of it, needs to come from you. Like everybody, you'll have good days and bad days, but most of all, you'll learn. But don't underestimate how much you bring to the table and how much the outcome is down to what you say, feel or do.

Unconsciously, your real beliefs can drive the outcome. If you secretly think deep down it won't work or it won't happen to you, this will leak out. You'll ask leading questions that are negatively geared to presenting the situation as not being possible and give the other person the opportunity to pass.

If you are sceptical, it will show in the little things that you do; the micro-expressions, how you hold yourself, and how you hesitate, which all manifest to create the outcome that you believe will happen. It's just like a self-fulfilling prophecy.

If that sounds like you and you're reading this, thinking that's easy for you to say, but deep down that doesn't happen to me. You're right! It doesn't happen to you, and won't happen until you change your mindset.

Your mindset is capable of unlocking the situation before it even happens. As we've spoken about previously, this is our most powerful tool. Visualisation is another core concept because knowing how you will respond in a situation is so important. When your 'If then' plans work and happen automatically, you intuitively go into autopilot.

I've seen it time and time again; someone half-heartedly wants to get a deal. They'd like a certain thing to happen but they are subtly telling themselves all the time that it won't happen. Listen to the story that you are telling yourself. If this is you, and you'll know if it is, then be honest and just accept that you have been holding yourself back from the possibility.

Why?

It doesn't matter why. It could have been how you were brought up, what you were taught to believe, how you protect yourself from disappointment, or a mechanism for control.

Whatever the reason is, it doesn't matter; what matters is that you understand how incredibly important your belief system is and how it holds the key to moving forward.

Once you tap into your belief system, the charisma, the joy, the passion and the motivation will all be released enough to make it happen. You will be aligned. When your goals and values are aligned for success, anything is possible. This alignment is the driving force. You are no longer are you at odds with yourself or holding yourself back. You don't internally question your actions or hesitate; you are just in the moment. You are at one with the situation and you bring flow. This is when your 'you' comes out.

It's like when you are talking to your best friend and time flies as you're just in the moment, having the best time. You are in your element because you are aligned with yourself internally and acting from your true north. Your inner self is completely happy with your actions, words and behaviours.

Getting the same alignment for negotiations is extremely important. It's the key to what can happen and what you believe can happen, which are intrinsically linked. You'll already know people in your life, maybe even your friends, colleagues or family members, whose steps just seem to fall into place and their world just seems to offer them opportunity. This is because they are aligned with what they want internally.

8.2 How to Negotiate When the Other Side Has More Power

This is one of those frequently asked questions and a hot topic for anyone who is looking to improve their negotiation skills.

To understand how power transcends all manner of negotiations and the influence that it has on the decision-making process, we must first understand what it is and where it comes from.

Power is defined by Robert A Dahl (1957) as: 'A has power over B to the extent that he can get B to do something B would not otherwise do'. Dahl's definition captures the relational dynamic of power, treating it as something of a 'fixed resource' that can be directed at will. Dahl was a politically theorist and Sterling professor at Yale University who made major contributions to the understanding of democracy.

In negotiation, however, we know that power, like beauty, lies in the eye of the beholder. As they say, perception really is the co-pilot to reality and in the case of power it takes it this saying to a whole new level. This is the reason that start-ups align themselves with larger corporates, because of the perceived power this brings in the market and the additional clout they can dish out in a negotiation.

For a negotiation related definition, we should look to Zartman and Rubin's definition, which is based on their studies. They define power as 'the perceived capacity of one side to produce an intended effect on another through a move that may involve the use of resources'.

The keyword in this definition is *perceived*; for example, the ability of one party to influence another through the strategic positioning of a product by highlighting its strengths or a core competitor advantage within a portfolio, rather than focusing on the broader company as a whole entity.

The first question to ask is, do they actually have more power or is it just perceived?

Power is a funny thing; it can be there one minute and gone the next. It can be given and taken away, possessed and then lost. I want to point out here that we are talking about transactional power, such as the authority that comes from being in a position of power. We are not talking about power that comes from within, like willpower or belief. Power as a structural concept can either be symmetric (where both sides have equal power) or asymmetric (where there is an imbalance of power). There are also different types of structural power that derive from a position of power, like an authority figure (e.g. a police officer). This is also called legitimate power (e.g. an expert). Authority figures command respect and induce compliance, and are also open to exploitation. If you've seen the Netflix original series, *Narcos*, you'll have more of an idea of how this works.

Power used as a strategy through coercion, intimidation or threats is a bad idea, as inflicting power on someone typically provokes the use of power in retaliation. However, in some scenarios power can be used to create opportunities for mutual gain. Thompson promotes the use of 'enlightened power' in this scenario. Negotiators 'get a bigger slice of the pie by creating a larger pie'. Again, this approach comes down to – you guessed it – influence. If a smaller entity can influence and direct the attention of a larger, more powerful entity, for the purposes of mutual gain by expanding the size of the prize through previously untapped avenues, then all credit to you. You see this type of 'enlightened power' occurs in politics all the time, where previously untouched areas become areas of interest seemingly overnight. Whereas, behind the scenes, persistent lobbying is taking place to highlight the mutual benefit.

The phrase 'look how the tables have turned' is often used to describe a shift in power that no one could see coming due to changes in situational factors. Now we have established that power is a kinetic element in the process of negotiation, the question is how and what causes a shift in power?

To understand this, it's important to understand the factors that cause the deterioration of communication and the breakdown of the negotiation, so that they can be avoided like the plague.

The first is information scarcity; this occurs in situations where some variables or information is simply unknown. For instance, this could be sales revenue in the future, although projections of estimated revenue can be made there is still an element of the unknown. Other examples could include economic disaster or competitor advancement through discovery, mergers and acquisitions, changes in legislation and the death of a CEO. Information scarcity is not something that you either have or you don't have in your negotiations; it's a spectrum, and each negotiation you go into will be somewhere along that spectrum in its degree of scarcity, which ranges from known to unknown. Therefore, when we think about best practices, it's important to think about the amount of unknown information in the negotiation. Becoming aware of this allows both parties to aim to reduce this gap and go through a process of discovery.

The second element that causes the power to shift is information asymmetry. This occurs when one side has either more or higher quality information than the other. This creates an imbalance of power. Again, world-class negotiators should recognise this imbalance of power and seek to use this awareness of its presence as a strategic method of trust building by reducing the information asymmetry gap.

To give these factors a more real-world applicability in the context of a likely negotiation scenario where they would appear, let's use the example of a start-up negotiating for funding with a venture capitalist (VC). The start-up, naturally due to its proximity, holds more and higher quality information than the VC about the product it has created. When it comes to the bargaining process, the combination of both information scarcity and information asymmetry is what causes many negotiations to grind to a halt.

As with most high stakes negotiations, there are also multiple variables at play here. The start-up is pitching the opportunity to invest in it in return for the acquisition of equity stake, which is derived from a hypothesised valuation based on a number of assumptions. The ultimate agreement that needs to be reached is about how much this company is worth and how much do I get in return for my investment?

From the VC's perspective, another hugely important factor is the exit, as it will only make good on the investment if the start-up successfully exits, typically through either IPO or acquisition.

Therefore, the VC needs to consider a multitude of factors, such as its ability to add value through its network, expertise and capital, as well as the realised and potential capabilities of the product, the founders and, of course, the size of the target market. All these things need to be appropriately weighed up when the VC is negotiating terms with the start-up.

On the flipside, you have the ambitious start-up, who believes they will go all the way and become the next big thing. They are looking to downplay the risks and upsell the opportunity without giving too much away in return for the required capital investment. Any equity they do give away will dilute their own stake in the business and could cost them millions of dollars further down the line if they become successful.

It's an interesting dynamic at play, and as you can start to see, the picture becomes crowded and there's a multitude of factors that need to be taken into consideration, even with this basic storyline. If you add to this increased information scarcity, information asymmetry and the imbalance of power, it is a recipe for disaster if the process is not carefully managed.

Countless research studies tell us that entrepreneurs tend to be far more overly optimistic compared to our cautious investors. Interestingly, research by Graebner has also shown that entrepreneurs trust investors more than investors trust them, which is partly to do with the flow of money and partly with the overly optimistic outlook.

The investor's mindset is biased towards the belief that the entrepreneur is seeking to hide information. It also leans towards 'value maximising' strategies and is prone to risk-taking behaviours that will ultimately reduce their rate of return.

Statistics show that a significant number of start-ups fail to get funding due to a breakdown in the negotiation.

The dynamic between the investor and the entrepreneur is much like that of a young couple on a date. Each is trying to figure out, *is this for real, do I trust you, do I see potential in this relationship, will it go all the way*?

The interesting thing is that both sides need each other to make it a successful partnership, much like a relationship. Without it they have nothing. The interplay between the entrepreneur's over-confidence and the investor's scepticism results in a tug of war that has the capacity to derail the whole negotiation.

The upshot is that both parties form substantially different valuations of the start-up leading to, in many cases, a full breakdown of the negotiation.

Complex problem + Information scarcity/asymmetry = Lack of trust/frustration = Breakdown of negotiation.

8.3 Bargaining and Assumptions

Studies have shown that the bedrock of negotiations between the corporate financier and entrepreneurs rests at the intersection of trust and information sharing.

In order to both decrease the risk of the entrepreneur using deception and reduce the information asymmetry gap that exists between the two parties, the process of information exchange must occur in an interactive bargaining process.

In this example, research shows that information sharing and discussion are both needed. If the start-up and the investor can switch their attention away from the overall valuation figure to discuss *how* the actual valuation was formed, they will increase the opportunity for successful negotiation.

By entering into discussion around the *assumptions* made on either side, the opportunity for understanding and effective communication can take place. It is thought that if the other side can understand *why* the assumptions were made in the way that they were, then it is more likely to build trust. A more successful outcome is achieved because a relationship is formed when trust is built through this information exchange process.

The solution to this type of negotiation, however, can be applied to any number of situations where you have two semi-opposing mindsets and an imbalance of power due to asymmetric information.

The investor and entrepreneur have a greater probability of striking a deal by focusing on the assumptions that were made and why (e.g. projected cash flow, sales forecasts, rate of return) and then explaining their needs, values and viewpoints.

1. Because the exchange of information increases the understanding of each other's mindset, point of view and thinking. Any process by which we can gain a greater understanding of the other party's take on things is valuable.

2. By going through each assumption that has been made, they have the opportunity to negotiate at a granular level. By diving into the specifics of how they came up with the number they did, rather than focusing on the overall valuation figure itself, the entrepreneur and investor can move forward, the wheels of the negotiation can start to turn and micro-agreements can be made. As James Sebenius previously told us, focus on the details when a deal has reached deadlock.

By understanding the assumptions and thinking on a deeper level, we can resolve the asymmetry of information. This reduces the lack of trust and frustration and, therefore, decreases the risk of failure to reach a deal.

So you can see how breaking this problem down to its core components in detail can aid the negotiation process, reduce the information asymmetry and restore the balance of power.

This is important because it's easy in life to focus only on our own perspective and not consider what the other side might be thinking or where they are coming from. Spending time thinking about the other side's perspective, and what they know and don't know, should form part of the preparation process used in any negotiation.

8.4 Anchoring

When we talk about anchoring, we are talking about controlling the outcome of the negotiation by presenting subtle cues to influence the boundaries. For instance, I could walk into the room and state I want a 50% discount because that's what we get from our competitors. Or I could say, I only have 30 minutes to complete the deal. Or, last year we made $1 million in sales revenue, this year I need you to make $1.5 million. Each one of these details is an anchor point that steers the negotiation and leads people to believe and work within the constraints of these defined goals. Anchoring ignores the context and can be a tool in negotiation to psychologically position a deal to look more favourable, simply by setting the bar higher to begin with and then accepting a lower offer.

8.5 Cold Calling

Let's not get our knickers in a twist over this one; cold calling is a pretty awesome skill to have in your back pocket. It's the ability to go from A-Z in a matter of minutes. So what are some of the cold calling tactics that can increase effectiveness and open more doors?

- If possible, go straight to the source; get the direct phone number of the person you are trying to call rather than going through a reception desk. If you can't get the direct line, then ask for it before they transfer you through; that way you can skip that step and have more control over the communication efforts.

- Once you connect, you have about five seconds to make the other person feel at ease and understand the purpose. My style is to open up with a friendly, 'Hello Jim, it's Tim here from AutoTyres.' 'Hey Tim, how are you?' 'I'm good thanks, I wanted to give you a call regarding our newest packages as I think we could work well together, do you have time now for a quick chat?' This gives them the option to say no. If it is a no, then reschedule the call for later in the day. If it's a yes, give some more context and keep it light and positive. Touch on the key details of value (cost saving, additional revenue, new business etc), then if it's relevant, get a time in the diary to meet up and explore more.

- Don't be afraid to pick up the phone. It's just a phone call; stop focusing on yourself and focus on the mutual value that you can create by making contact. If they don't want to hear about it when you connect you're not going to force them, so be friendly, explain your purpose, make it sound like you're chatting to a friend, rather than reading from a script. We're going for natural and relaxed here, rather than stressful and pressured.

- Create your own momentum. I find the best way to get into a cold calling sprint is to line up a number of calls (5-10) that I want to make and then do them all, one after the other. This creates a sense of momentum and allows you to move on from one conversation to the next with a sense of purpose. I love cold calling as a technique for opening doors, making things happen or getting meetings in the diary, as there's a sense of unlimited possibility about it. The other great thing about having a list is you can end the conversation and move on to the next call if someone is particularly grumpy when you call them or start giving you a hard time. The key is to be as low touch as needed unless the conversation opens up into more. You're not going to sit around being disrespected, nor are you going to go into the conversation thinking that people are out to get you. It's a balance between creating the conversation you want to have and knowing when to pull the plug.

- LinkedIn, Facebook and emails are all tools for your deployment; utilise them to make initial contact. We are in a golden age where we are more connected in more ways than ever before, so as it's a travesty not to use this advantage.

Let's get social

Having said that, let's delve into a few of the tools that we can use to open doors, create negotiation opportunities and enhance our success in cold calling.

LinkedIn

What a tool, the savvy hunter is a wiz at LinkedIn. There's so much information and so many opportunities for common ground all in one place. LinkedIn gives you more than just the current title and place of employment; it gives you someone's journey, including their interests, associations and mutual connections. If we think about networking in the 21st century, then this is a melting pot of resource at your fingertips.

In 2012, LinkedIn introduced a new product called Sales Navigator. It's primary purpose is for large corporates to increase the opportunity for introductions and give a holistic view of the sales team's actions, such as in-mails, searches and activity on LinkedIn.

The real value I see here is that it gives access to your private network. A little feature called Teamlink allows you to see the connections that your colleagues have, even if you aren't 1st degree connected to them. This works well in the sales arena. If, for example, you are trying to reach the CMO for a specific company and can see that someone in your finance department has a 1st degree connection, then we are onto a win.

First off, this gives you the opportunity to probe for more information. Uncovering more information and gaining insights should be your primary focus here, and then if the other person feels comfortable and it would be appropriate, then by all means go for the personal introduction. This is how social media is creating massive value in business and negotiation in the 21st century. In an interview for *MIT Sloan Management Review*, Ralf Vonsonsen, Head of Marketing for LinkedIn, calls it 'Social Selling'. The paper goes into detail discussing the shift towards this technique and it is aptly entitled, *How Social Selling is Reinventing Cold Calling*:

It's really utilising all of the fantastic data that's out there that helps us to make us visible to the connections and relationships we have. We can take this data and combine it with the branding and information that we as professionals are sharing, and create both a more meaningful experience and conversation.

Vonsonsen also says that when it's done well, social selling 'moves our contact from a traditional cold call to either a warm introduction or at least a warm conversation'.

LinkedIn has become a platform for valued introductions and making the initial first contact. We are in a world of possibility right now and it has never been easier to both get in contact with those whom we admire – leaders with influence – and advance our ambitions, all in one place.

Emails

To explain this better, I am going to reference the work of my main man Adam Grant, who has written a number of posts on the components of 'cold emails' that make them both effective and polite. Through a combination of his own research and experience, Adam has found that he replies faster to some emails than others. He outlines six principles that he uses to elicit faster replies to emails.

1. Perfect the subject line – inspire Curiosity, Utility or Both.
2. Tell them why you chose them – Adam states that: 'Good emails overcome this barrier by highlighting what drew you to this person and the distinctive value that he or she can add.'

3. Show them you have done your homework – people want to see that you've put some effort into your request.

4. Highlight uncommon commonalities – this goes back to leveraging the tools at your disposal, like LinkedIn, to find those rare pastimes that you have in common with the person you are trying to connect with. If you've read Adam's book, *Give and Take,* you'll know that rare similarities 'allow us to standout and fit in at the same time'.

5. Make your requests specific and keep them short and sweet.

6. Express gratitude. This is a double win. One of Adam's studies has shown that not only do emails containing the words, 'Thank you so much! I am really grateful', double your chances of getting a response, they also boost helping rates from 25%-55%. You do the maths! It's a no-brainer.

If you can't tell already, I love Adam's work.

WhatsApp

The game has changed now that WhatsApp is commonplace on the negotiating scene. It is frequently used in politics and diplomacy due to its speed, functionality and connectivity. The EU reportedly uses it to engage and arrange huddles, discuss strategy and gauge the feeling in the room. It's been tailor-made for diplomacy; you don't even have to leave the room.

'You can form small groups of like-minded allies, take photos of annotated documents, ask people what they think without the whole room knowing,' a senior Western diplomat said.

With 1.2 billion people on WhatsApp, including 175 million daily active users and 42 billion messages sent daily, it's a negotiator's new best friend. Since April 2016, security has not been an issue either, as it's got end-to-end encryption meaning that 'you can send a more secure message through WhatsApp now than most government information systems,' according to Jon Alterman, a former state department policy planning staff official, who is now senior vice-president at the Centre for Strategic and International Studies.

This is also about influence, as you can set up chat groups of like-minded peers. The rules of the game have changed and influencing people and developing face-to-face relationships is no longer just about physical contact to; it's now gone digital.

Welcome to 21st century negotiation. Gaining influence used to be all about who you knew and bending their ear so that they could see your point of view, but now it's decided by the WhatsApp group you are a part of.

In addition to being a tool that can organise huddles, talk tactics and agree deals when other key decision-makers can't be in the room, WhatsApp is also used as a means of controlling the course of the negotiation, debate or the direction of the conversation. Representatives can be instructed to interrupt, discuss certain topics, push certain agendas, and avoid others while they are communicating in real-time during a tough negotiation.

So long for the pre-negotiation catch up. WhatsApp is a game changer and one we can use to our advantage, as well as be aware of.

WhatsApp allows the negotiation to cross borders with ease, whether we are negotiating with silent partners, in different time zones or involving multiple parties all at once.

Emoji

This creates an emotional connection, lightens the mood and brings the human touch to the negotiating table. Strategic use of emojis in online negotiations can, if used correctly, tap into that human element in a virtual environment. In an online environment, negotiation messages are open to being misconstrued. This is where emojis can help to express and clarify emotions and their meanings. Emojis are an evolution of language. In 2015, the first ever emoji was entered into the Oxford Dictionary, *Face with Tears of Joy*. Also known as the LOL emoji, it made up nearly 20% of all emoji use in the UK in 2015, according to SwiftKey.

8.6 How to Negotiate with Hackers

Data breaches, hackers and cyber security are all highly relevant topics in today's digitally savvy world. With the rise of ransomware, 'a type of malicious software from cryptovirology that threatens to publish the victim's data or perpetually block access to it unless a ransom is paid', negotiation with hackers has become increasingly commonplace. Ransomware can be bought on the darknet, which is 'any overlay network that can be accessed only with specific software, configurations, or authorisation, often using non-standard communications protocols and ports', with relative ease and at low cost.

Malwarebytes, a cyber security and anti-malware firm, estimates that 40% of companies worldwide have been targeted by a ransomware attack (August 2016). In Britain, the figure is estimated to be as high as 54% and a study of 500 companies across four countries found that 33% of them had lost revenue as a result of a malware attack. It can be expensive too, with 3% of attacks demanding upwards of $50,000.

Interestingly though, the Malwarebytes study also indicates that there are differences between countries as to who pays up and who doesn't. In the UK, it's estimated that 50% of businesses end up coughing up the charges demanded, which is in contrast to the US, where they found that 97% of businesses resist paying. Cue an overly polite British scene, with Hugh Grant confronting the cyber criminals and then opening up his wallet, saying, 'Oh right, I see, how would you like payment? Is cash alright, old chap?' I jest.

There have been a number of explanations for these differences; namely it's thought that one third of British businesses don't back up their data, so they're forced to pay up as a means of gaining access to files that would be otherwise destroyed. The problem is that payments made to attackers may inadvertently be funding other types of criminal activities, let alone fuelling the fire for more attacks.

This is a very real scenario for many of today's top executives and members of the public. The professional negotiator and CEO and founder of Nest, Moty Cristal, explained why negotiation is vital in these situations while speaking at the WIRED 2016 security conference. Nest is a professional consultancy that provides negotiation support and assistance to senior executives who are facing complex negotiation challenges, like crisis management and training. Nest aims to achieve a results-oriented negotiation process on both a strategic and tactical level. While exploring what's on offer for an executive at Nest, I found that many of the topics are incredibly enticing and not dissimilar to what we are covering in this book (e.g. complete mapping of the relevant organisation systems, psychological profiling, building relevant and appropriate negotiation teams, designing your negotiation strategy and improving alternatives). I focus your attention on these to show you that the same careful planning and structure around negotiation is required at any level, whether this is around the team doing the negotiating, the preparation or the strategy.

Moty described one scenario where the CEO of a financial institution got an interesting email entitled 'open this Ronny'. The executive opened up the email to see sensitive customer-related information. Then, two minutes after opening it, he got a message on his WhatsApp, saying: 'That was a small tip of the iceberg, hopefully those proofs are sufficient so far.' Then came the demand.

'Our demand is a single non-negotiable payment of 500 bitcoins (worth $120,000 at the time) without any further sanction from our side. So far, we only extracted the data without damaging it or trading it. This could be real-world penetration testing or an event that will damage your brand in an irreversible way. Just think what a leak of all that on the relevant forums, an article on xxxx and other places could do.'

'But that was not the last message," Moty continued. 'The final message read, we don't want you to end up like Ashley Maddison CEO, this is not a personal matter J'

Moty, who is an expert in hostage negotiations, says they're easier to negotiate because you speak with the bad guys, and then at the end of the day, if all else fails, you have the SWAT team with you and the situation comes to an end one way or another.

'But what happens in the virtual world when your data is being held hostage? How do you negotiate that?' he asked the audience rhetorically.

Moty outlined three rules to follow in any cyber extortion negotiation. These are:

1. **Respect** – the hacker should be treated with professional respect at all times. This comes down to the quality of information the hacker holds. They hold the cards; the negotiator does not. The hacker knows what they have; the negotiator is trying to piece together the jigsaw piece by piece.
2. **Coordinate** – make sure the entire crisis team are synchronised; 'a professional negotiator will have to navigate these different actors, who sometimes have different interests'.
3. **Adjust** – adapt to the rapid pace of the cyber extortion negotiations. The longer the negotiation takes, the higher the hacker's risk of exposure.

Moty is a big fan of the human element in negotiation and states that he 'strongly believes that managing the human factor is key to overcoming a cyber crisis'. He goes on to explain the steps that he takes to negotiate with cyber criminals; so listen up, this is how the pros do it.

1. **Profiling** – who am I dealing with? How do they do this? You start to communicate with the other side. They write to me. What are their motivations and incentive? Throughout the early stages of the process, you try to build up a profile of who you are dealing with.
2. **Assess the cost of 'no deal'** – this informs whether you should pay or not. Funnily enough, the other side may try to explain the cost of no deal to you

(e.g. you are a public company, you don't want this sensitive customer information leaked). They will try to explain why you should pay them. He then introduces 'The Board tactic', saying: 'I can't agree to that; the board didn't agree'. Throughout the two-month long process, he kept on referring to 'The Board'. Moty states, 'This is important, because 60% of negotiations failures can be attributed not to failure to get a deal, but to failure to coordinate internally. This is the gap between the negotiator and the decision maker.' Moty explains that he spends most of his time mediating between the CEO and the main shareholder who says, 'I will not be extorted.' He states that, 'Managing the internal dynamic is really a challenge.'

3. **Flexibilities** – Throughout the process he tries to establish flexibilities and bargains for a discount. He states that if you get a 'no', the answer shouldn't be 'Why not, you should do it.' Instead, the answer in negotiation should be, 'If not that, then what yes?'

4. **Negotiate for time** – Why? So that the techies can trace back exactly what has been stolen. It's here that he does 'The Move', which is controlling the negotiation process by framing the outcomes (e.g. six payments, once the first is made, you share with me the inventory of what you have from us, which means that: 'I'm not paying the ransom until you give me something in return'). See below.

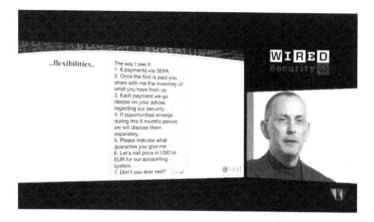

*See the last point on the list, 'Don't you ever rest?' This is 'the personal connection'.

5. **Move towards a deal** – Then start to bargain. 'My friends, this has now moved from a ransom, to a deal,' Moty continues. He explains that this is often a crucial step, given the tension of the board and how keen they are to ensure that the data is not sold to a competitor.

Ultimately, he explains that cyber extorters operate with a criminal code of ethics and he uses this to negotiate the deal. His final resounding point is 'that at the end of the day, it is the human factor that needs to be managed with the technological elements'. You see in the above example that both a WhatsApp emoji and the human touch were instrumental in facilitating the dialogue.

Symantec estimates that over $4 billion was paid to hackers in 2013 and reports indicate that the figure has increased in the years since then. The reality is that cyber extortion is a very real situation that increasing numbers of companies and individuals find themselves in. The situation requires experienced handling and 'structured process design', as Moty refers to it. It's easy to see how mistakes in the decision-making process are made, with individuals opening themselves up to further manipulation because they assume that dealing with hackers is just like dealing with anyone else or a disgruntled customer. We are talking about a situation here that combines high levels of uncertainty, internal blame games and conflicting motivates. It's one choppy sea to navigate.

Summary

- When the other side has more power, look for the differences
- Anchor to create invisible boundaries, watch out for when the other side uses anchors to steer the negotiation
- WhatsApp, Emoji and social media are now commonplace in negotiations and are used as tools to enhance the speed of negotiation and information exchange
- Data security is of the upmost importance; negotiation has crossed into new territories

Activity

In this activity, I want to show you that anything is possible. I want you to construct an email by using Adam's 6 steps that are to be sent to a person who inspires you. This must be someone you consider to be out of reach from your normal circle of influence. Ideally, they will be someone of great importance to your life and there will be a purpose to your communication. Once you have perfected your email, hit send and let me know via my Facebook page whether you receive a response. To help you with this, there is also a link in the resources section to another of my favourite articles by Adam Grant, *9 steps not to appear rude*. Good luck and don't forget to share what happens with me on Facebook, Twitter or my website.

PART 5

REAL-WORLD NEGOTIATION EXAMPLES

9

IT'S SHOW TIME
PART 1: YOUR HOME AND CAREER

'Don't tell people your dreams, show them.'

OK, SO FAR, we've run through some of the core concepts of successful negotiation. We've looked at stamina and mental toughness, the importance of going for it and when to do so, and the underlying goal of win-win negotiations. Now it's time to get serious; what about the big game?

I'm talking about when it really matters. This includes things like buying a house or a new car, or that promotion at work you've been after. In this chapter, I'll break down what you need to know about when you go into any one of these situations, and also how to deliver the best outcome. The message I hope you're getting is that negotiation is a tool that can help you to get more of what you want and build a life of endless possibility.

9.1 Buying a House or Flat

Depending on where you live, there will be different rules for how the real estate process is completed. For instance, if you're from Down Under, then purchasing a house is more likely be done in the form of an auction. If you live in Blighty, it will most likely be conducted through a series of in-person showings by a real estate agent who acts as the go conduit between the seller's agent and you.

Whatever your situation, and regardless of where you live, the principles I am about to share can still be applied to help you secure a more valuable deal.

First off, you need to decide who will go to the initial house viewing with you. Will you go alone or will it be you and your partner? Will your mother in-law be attending, or perhaps your dad? These are important details because the more people we bring into the mix, the more variables we need to control. It's also important because you need to know who's going to leak telltale signs to the real estate agent when you know you've found the perfect abode. The more people are involved, the more chance there is of leakage. It's as simple as that.

When you do find that perfect house, it's only natural to be excited and initial reactions may involve you shouting the house down and screaming, 'THIS IS IT! This is the one, we've found it!' If this is you, then halt! Cease this behaviour now; control your bad self! Please do yourself a favour and don't go back to the inspection after you have decided it is the one, unless you are completely sure that you can control yourself.

This type of reaction has the potential to cost you thousands of dollars. If you happen to find the perfect house, and you just can't hold back the excitement – keep this inside you until you are off the property and have a chance to review the details in the privacy of your own home.

Any giveaway like this will only serve to give the real estate agent more of an inside scoop on how badly you want it, and if this is revealed you are increasing the leverage they have on you. Agents work for commission through making sales. This is not a bad thing and can be swung to your advantage; however, screaming the house down that you want the place is like you're holding up a sign saying, 'Please charge me more, I am willing to pay the big bucks to secure this place.'

Like bees to honey, I guarantee it will damage any chances of a price reduction and make it harder to get a bargain. Therefore, it's mightily important that anyone viewing the property with you is also acutely aware of this and can temporarily control their emotional excitement until at least several miles away from the property.

Think of it like a job interview; when you score a higher salary than you were expecting, you don't suddenly jump up and start high fiving your new employers saying, 'That's great, thank you so much, I would have joined for less.' The same is true for house price negotiations. What's important is that you are willing to work with the letting agent. Once they see that the house alone won't get the deal across the line, they will work with you on the price, fees, furnishings, fittings, move-in dates and outdoor space to make the deal more attractive.

The fact that estate agents work on sales commission is a beautiful thing but you need it to work for you, not against you. So once you find a place you like and have a set budget in mind; then they can work on your behalf to get the commission and talk with the seller to bring the price down and get the deal over the line.

Ultimately, they're going to want a sale to go through; not to bag out estate agents. There will be some that do the right thing and won't push you to pay more than you can afford, and on the flip side there will also be those who take you for a pretty penny if you let them. It is important that you find someone who's going to respect your boundaries and understands it's their job to find you a suitable property where there's potential to get it over the line within your budget.

It's important that you are also realistic with what you can get for your money in the desired area; the old menu trick of showing you something amazing and over budget first and then something within budget will play on your mind. There's also proven evidence of both primacy and regency effect taking hold here; the fact that we are more likely to remember what we first and last see rather than the stuff in the middle. Be careful of these tricks; remember that you are potentially more emotional when you are in the house-buying process and so are more open to manipulation.

Before going into any type of negotiation you need to know the market realities. Assessing market demands from a homeowner's perspective will to give you a sense of how hard you can negotiate.

How are houses selling in the local area? What is economic sentiment currently like? Are more people shifting towards renting and away from buying? Is there a trend towards foreign investment? Who is buying? Who is selling? Why are they selling, what are their motivations? These general trends will outline some very important information as to how to structure your negotiation.

9.2 House Auctions

When it comes to auctions, emotions are usually high, which leads to overpayment. If you are in this type of situation for a property you feel you must have, it is probably better to get in there first and try to take it off the market before it goes up for auction. That way you can secure the asset at the cost you are willing to pay without getting involved with a high stakes emotional game on the day of the auction. We talked about emotion and negotiation in Chapter 3 and this is unfortunately one of those situations where you need to be strategic, know your limits and leave emotion at the door (pardon the new dad joke).

Again, it is important to manage the information you share at a negotiation as you don't know who the other potential buyers are and who might turn out be your biggest competition. Therefore, you should refrain from disclosing any information about your maximum price, what you think the property is worth and anything that would suggest how badly you want the property. Think of it like a game of poker; keep your cards close to your chest. It might sound simple, but so many people forget these principles in the heat of the moment and it can end up costing them heavily.

So, we've talked about managing your emotions; up next is clarity. It's super important that you clearly outline your ideal price and at the same time keep in mind your walk away price. The skill is in the journey you take between the two prices in relation to market information, emotional pressures and the information you receive from the letting agent. Be mindful that your gut instinct needs to be trusted in this instance. The letting agency plays a pivotal role in how the negotiation plays out between you, 'the buyer', and the owner, 'the seller'.

Keep your Zone of Possible Agreement firmly planted in your mind; this is your bargaining range. Once the auction goes outside of this range, it's time to walk away.

Ryan Serhant and Fredrik Eklund from Bravo's *Million Dollar Listing New York* are experts in the field who can so eloquently read their audience. Understanding other people's motivations is key. If you can find out why the homeowner is selling and how quickly they want to sell, then you are suddenly in pole position as this is very valuable information. If you find out they need a quick sale because they are moving abroad for a job opportunity and have no time to waste, you can bet your bottom dollar they would be open to a sensible offer upfront rather than waiting to find out what the market thinks at auction. 'A bird in the hand,' as they say.

So read people, read the signs, and find out how many other people have viewed the property. It's all about asking open questions that uncover information and using closed questions to confirm specific detail. Buying a house is like chasing a girl you have a crush on; if you really want to get the girl, you must play it cool. Not too cool that you don't show any interest, but just enough that she knows, is intrigued and comes closer. That's when you ask her out, on her terms rather than in front of everyone on yours.

Buying a house is a fun process and should be enjoyed. It's one of the few times in our lives we get to spend a vast amount of money on something that sets us up for the future and provides memories and even a legacy for years to come. It's important to make the right choice. When you know, you know; just don't let them know that you know and you'll walk into a good spot for the negotiation. Be clear and say upfront: 'We'd like to make an offer'.

9.3 Negotiating a Pay Increase

When people find out that my specialist area is negotiation, nine times out of ten the first question they ask is, how do I best negotiate a pay rise?

As we've already discussed throughout this book, negotiating isn't about pulling the wool over someone's eyes. It's about demonstrating and positioning value in a way that makes a desired outcome more possible.

Pay rises can be a big one because they matter, and because of this they tend to be surrounded by emotion, which can lead us off track.

When I went into my first pay rise negotiation, I learned a valuable lesson that has stayed with me ever since. I didn't have all the facts, I wasn't prepared and I didn't influence the direction of the conversation. It wasn't even a conversation I had pushed for, but that doesn't make it right that I found it difficult to provide tangible hard metrics to support my rationale. I found myself sitting in front of a group of senior leaders being asked to describe why I wanted a pay rise. It's a fair question and one that I have made sure I can answer at a moment's notice ever since. Like anything in this sphere of negotiation, whether it's title changes, pay increases or changes to role responsibilities, it's paramount to be prepared and have a map in your mind of where you want to go.

My biggest piece of advice on this is be able to demonstrate your value with actual hard facts and results. Think about it from their point of view; if they can pay you the same or someone else the same to get the same results, then why should they pay you more?

If the conversation falls outside of the normal cycle for reviews, then the company may have budgetary constraints to consider, as well as a need for further proof and motivation if they are to take the request seriously. Think BATNA.

So how do we handle this? You've been called into the room and asked point blank, 'Why do you want a pay rise?' What you must now do is demonstrate specific value and be very clear about how you have driven dollars to their bottom line. If you can demonstrate tangible results you are halfway there. The key is to remain calm. Ideally, you will have been tracking your specific results for the past few months and be able to show them physical evidence in the form of a spreadsheet or have three well-prepared case studies that clearly articulate where you have gone above and beyond for the company, exceeding what you are paid for.

Please don't just state things that are within your job description; this is what you are paid to do already. You need to be involved in tasks and producing results that are above your current position and fall outside the remit of everyday business.

People can find themselves getting stuck in pay rise negotiations because they are focusing on what they need. 'I need a pay rise because I want to put my kids into a better school.' 'I want to pay for my honeymoon,' or 'pay off the car loan'.

I understand if this is where you are coming from, I really do. But how do these things benefit the business that is paying you, apart from making your life more manageable?

Please try to think of it from the perspective of the business. The business may very well want to pay you more money based on exceptional results, but they are a business and so will only do it if it makes sense commercially.

They may also want to see you demonstrate the business case for doing so. The business is there to succeed; therefore, you need to demonstrate how you will help them to do that and the additional value you will be adding.

The second point I recommend is timing; make sure you are having the right conversation at the right time. It is one thing to have the courage to go and discuss a pay rise with your boss, it's another to find the right time. Making sure you have picked the right time is another 25% of the way there.

So now we've got 75% of the conversation covered; what else can impact on its success?

Ah, glad you asked friends. Here's a list of questions you need to think deeply about to ensure you are going to have a successful conversation.

Do your research and think about your options.

- Are you truly undervalued right now?
- Are you committed; do you like your current job?
- Can you execute; can you do what you say you are going to do?
- What is on your boss' mind right now?
- What do you think your boss will say?
- Will this be a surprise to them?
- What is the state of the business right now?
- Are they hiring or firing?

Let's looks at these quickly in more detail.

Are you truly undervalued? This question speaks to market rates, company rates and overall satisfaction, based on the perceived quality of the job you have been doing.

Do you like your current job? Vibes are contagious; it's very easy to pick up on if someone is happy in their job. If you're not happy, it's likely you haven't been performing to your highest potential. That's not to say you've been doing badly and there aren't valid reasons for your feelings. It's just important to note where you are on a scale of 1-10 (1 lowest happiness, 10 over the moon) so that you can be prepared if they ask you about this.

Can you do what you say you are going to do? This comes down to execution; there is no point in pushing for a pay rise if it hinges on the unattainable. It will be demotivating for you and for the company. People want to feel good, we all do. Therefore, it's important to put some achievable and realistic goals in place in an agreed upon time frame. Have you ever heard of SMART goals? What am I saying; of course you have. You are a go-getter. But just as a refresher, SMART goals are: Specific, Measurable, Achievable, Relevant and Time-Bound.

For example, I commit to bringing in $1.5 million in incremental revenue six months from this date.

What is on your boss' mind right now? This speaks to their mindset and timing. Does this exact moment correlate with a successful conversation or has she just come out of an important meeting and has an important presentation to deliver this afternoon. There can be any number of things that could lead to distraction. The key here is that you find a time to meet that works for both parties; not just for you because you want to get it off your chest and have been up all night thinking about this conversation.

We are only human, I get it, and there isn't always a perfect time. Like I said, this conversation can begin in the unlikeliest of places (at the bar, at a conference, on the commute to work) but just have a quick check and decide what's going on for your boss right now.

There is a link between the questions: 'What do you think your boss will say?' and 'Will this be a surprise for them?' These two probing questions bring into focus your emotional intelligence and awareness of the situation. If this conversation is likely to be a surprise for your boss or you don't think they will agree, it's worth checking in with yourself beforehand and running through these options in your mind so that you can control your emotions and handle objections with integrity if it happens.

Remember, this conversation doesn't have to be all or nothing. This can be the first of many that leads to greater things. An initial 'no' doesn't always mean 'no' and it can be a starting point to put yourself on the map, getting a specific goal-oriented plan in place to work towards an increase in remuneration.

What is the state of the business right now? Is the business going through significant change or is it relatively stable? This question allows you to gain a sense of the bigger picture, what's happening in other departments and across the business as a whole, including the market or field that your company operates in.

The market realities and challenges that the business faces are what senior leaders will be focused on; therefore, if you can demonstrate your understanding of these factors and how you can help navigate them you are on a potential path to success. Taking some time out to step off the dance floor (everyday business) and on to the balcony (away from the business, a place for deep thought) is a good habit to get into. You will be able to spot the areas of opportunity for the business by removing yourself from the day-to-day execution of business. This is a strategy for growth and it's a practice that senior business leaders engage in frequently. Often, it isn't until we stop and take time to step away from the habitual process of business that we can see the pockets of gold right in front of us, or have time to experience epiphanies.

Are they hiring or firing? This question begs another deeper question – why are they hiring or firing? Is it because they don't have headcount and are, therefore, letting people go, or are they growing at a rapid pace so that new roles are being added daily. It's good to have a sense of what the business is doing because if it is conducting either of these at scale, then it will likely come up in the conversation. Think of the business like an organism; it's either contracting or expanding, depending on market realities. To be in sync with the mindset of the business you need to look at why the business is undertaking certain activities.

Once you have answered these questions and have broken the situation down into manageable chunks, you next need to think about how you can make it easier for the business to agree to giving you a pay rise.

To do this you need to minimise their risk; an 'if/then' approach could be what you need.

For example, *if* I can bring in (x) dollars in new business by three months and sign up two new clients, can we agree that I would *then* warrant a pay rise of (y)?

It may seem like you are conceding here, but think of it from another perspective. If you are truly as good as you say you are, then you should have no problem delivering on what you've put forward. It may seem like you deserve the pay rise now but this is where a little patience pays off. If you desperately need the pay rise now and are truly undervalued, then it could be an opportunity and a sign that it's time to look elsewhere.

By linking your pay rise to specific results, benefits both parties. But remember that what you put forward must go above and beyond your normal KPIs. If you're a business development manager and your responsibility is to drive new business, then any agreement would need to reflect a significant uplift that can't be resourced from elsewhere.

If you deliver on these commitments and you find yourself in a scenario where they then don't uphold their end of the bargain, you will know it's time to move on and you'll have a great case study to take with you. The important thing to bear in mind is that contexts and markets change so quickly in the fast pace of business situations. What might be fine one day is outdated the next. Therefore, if this is a route you go down with all of the best intentions from both parties, it is still not guaranteed. Why? Because the business needs to operate at speed and make changes to its strategy to influence outcomes, and sometimes this impacts even the best laid plans.

That's why it's important to keep the time frame short (three to six months maximum), so that you can get measurable results and move forward with your request. There's no point it being an agreement to get a pay rise in a year or so; businesses change, economies change, mergers and acquisitions happen, people leave. What you are aiming for is a quick time frame to prove to them that you can deliver the goods.

The great thing in this win-win proposition is that you've taken the situation into your own hands rather than the alternative of 'hoping' that they notice all the new clients you have brought on board. A business is always going to look after its own needs and if they can get away with paying you less, they will do so. The key is to show them (rather than tell them) a plan of how you intend to demonstrate the value you bring in a specific and measurable way over a short time frame. Better yet, ask for feedback and work on the plan with your manager to make sure it aligns to their expectations. This takes the conversation to a new level; the level of action. It changes it from a 'you versus them' debate into a 'we are working together to achieve outcomes that are desirable for both parties'.

Lastly, stay humble. They don't have to pay you more. If it doesn't make sense to them as a business, don't be offended by this. Remember emotional criticism; world-class negotiators don't have time to get caught up in it. Businesses go through ebbs and flows, with different businesses having different cultures and different perspectives on remunerating, recognising and rewarding their staff. The best thing you can do through all of this is keep your integrity. At the end of the day, the business may not have enough in the kitty or may not want to pay you more, no matter what results you produce. Again, turn this insight into a positive; by having a well-prepared and data-driven conversation at the appropriate time, with the right people, you can get well-informed answers as to the possibility of a pay rise. If it's not going to happen, then you need to either make your peace with it, or start looking elsewhere; either way you are taking charge of your life and positioning yourself for success.

9.4 Negotiating the Salary in a New Job Offer

When applying for a new job, people often ask me when is the best time to start negotiating my salary? We touched on this earlier when we looked at how to structure the negotiation. Now let's focus on the other elements at play.

I look at it like this; firstly, you need to do some due diligence. Like with any negotiation, you need to know what's a good deal, what's an OK deal and what's sub-par.

Then you need to factor in your current situation.

- How long are you able to go without employment?
- Are you between jobs?
- Are you looking to switch industries?
- How much experience do you bring to the role?
- What can you learn from the role?
- What are the people like?
- What is the culture like?
- What does the company value?
- Where do you want to be in the role after this role?

There are a lot of questions you need to ask.

When I moved from media trading into advertising technology sales, I was taking on a completely new part of the industry. I based my job search not on salary, but on where I could learn the most and where could I have the most opportunity to work with people that were better than me at things I wanted to become good at.

That's why I didn't negotiate when the offer came through. A gasp, and I hear you say, 'but Tim you tell us to negotiate on everything'… true and I stand by that, but if you've set up the situation correctly, there should be little or no need to negotiate that much when the offer rolls around because the initial testing has already been carried out.

At some point during the interview process there will be a salary 'sense check' by either the recruiter or the employers themselves. They will ask what you are looking for in terms of salary expectations and they usually ask this early on to make sure you are on the same page and whether it's worth investing more time and money moving forward.

This is your cue to be bold and put it on the table. As I've mentioned before, this is where you need to say 20% higher than the salary you want. This is also the point where you need to lightly set some expectations for what else you want in the package; remember, it's not all about salary. I have found the best way to do this is by beginning the conversation by stating your expected base pay, then build on this with your expected bonus percentage. Then, lightly drop into the conversation some of the other benefits you are already receiving from your current employer or would expect to receive. By doing this, you are lightly peppering the conversation with little indicators that can later be brought into more direct discussion. You are sowing the seeds for future harvest and marinating the chicken for later consumption. OK, enough with the growth analogies; you get the idea.

There are a variety of perks that can be offered by a company that aren't in the form of salary and will save you a bucket load in the long run. These are benefits like car parking, free food, gym memberships, health insurance, holiday days, paternity and maternity leave, study leave, study fees, sick leave, training, pension, international travel, shares, equity, bonuses: these are all points of negotiation.

Here, though, you just need to articulate the figures and extras that you are looking for. This is a sense-checking exercise just to ensure that you are both on the same page. This is where you need to have courage, be strong and set your expectations out clearly and calmly.

This is not about being greedy; it's about presenting the facts based on the research you've already done. You know your value; you know your worth in the market and what typically comes with a job at this level. It's also the time to be aspirational and go for it.

When it comes to the final stages and they have made you an offer, you then have another opportunity to negotiate. This is where some people freak out and don't know what to do.

They are so happy that the offer has been made, and quite rightly. Interviewing for a job is a long and tiring process. You've come a long way, but 'whoa their nelly, hold your horses', let's just take a second to look at whether this deal offers fair value. If you have been consistent in communicating your expectations early on, then what they have offered you shouldn't be that far-off where you want to be. If that's the case, then ride on partner. If not, pick up the phone and have a chat about it. Ask if there's wiggle room on x, y and z. Reference the earlier conversation and use this to back up your points. Remember, the stronger your BATNA, the more leverage you have at this point.

The way I see it, you're worth whatever you think your worth. For example, if you think you can get a job that's paying $80k, but you only communicate that you'd like somewhere between $60-$80k, then chances are you'll end up with about $65k. It will be tough for you to get to the $80k mark. This is because the salary range is too large. It suggests you have a $20k discrepancy in what you think you are worth, and when you work this out that's a 33% difference in value (20/60), which is fairly large when we are talking about pay scales.

Remember the boundaries you set will act as signals to the employer/recruiter and this applies to any negotiation. Boundaries are signals and they directly influence the result.

If you want to get $100k you need to aim for the $95k-$110k position to make it easier for them to settle on $100k; better still, go in with $110k from the start. That way you are not framing it with an option that even includes $95k (below your ideal).

For every job, there's a sliding scale; it just depends on how you communicate it. Once you get the offer, you are in the driving seat; they have put an offer on the table and now you are able to fine-tune it.

If you think you are worth $100k, then say that from the get-go. Don't worry about it. If they've only got $80k, they'll find the cash if they want you. Whether the market agrees or not really comes down to how you deliver it, and most importantly, if you believe it. The next stage that builds on this is putting the meat on the bones – why do you deserve this level of pay? What is it that you are able to do that sets you apart and gives them (the recruiter/HR/manager) something to run with internally. After all, to set yourself up for success, they need to have a clear idea of why you deserve this salary. It doesn't just happen because you have the courage to ask for it.

What's important isn't so much whether you push for the $100k in isolation. What's important is that you've taken the time to ask yourself the right questions, like how badly do I need this job right now?

Get into the habit of assessing yourself and your needs on a regular basis, as getting real with your situation is a key skill to have. It will also make it easier for you to get into the headspace of their situation and close the gap between you and them finding a solution.

The problem people face is they leave all the negotiating to the end and then panic when the offer lands on the table. This is not the time to shock them with a list of demands as long as your arm. It will come across like you didn't expect to get the job; you were unprepared and aren't committed and, therefore, make the deal hard to get across the line.

People don't mind as long as they know where they stand; they will respect you for being able to clearly articulate your value. The focus should be less around what they are paying you and more around the fit for the team, the company culture and where bringing someone like you on could take the company to new levels.

When employers ask outright what people's salary expectations are, those who haven't done their due diligence will say the highest figure they think they can get away with. Emotions have a funny way of driving actions and when we are presented with an offer, it can be very easy to accept everything that's being said in the heat of the moment, until a few weeks later when you find out that everyone else has more holiday days, a car parking space close to work and a more favourable bonus structure. Don't kick yourself later; put in the time, do your research and have the conversation. Enjoy it, it doesn't need to be a topic that's not spoken about; after all, you are giving them a fair portion of your life to expand their business. Packages are just part of the process and a great part if done right and upfront from the beginning. Being consistent throughout the process is key here.

Professor Deepak Malhotra of Harvard Business School outlines 15 rules to abide by when negotiating a job offer:

1. **Don't underestimate likability** – when people like you, they will go in to bat for you. Often with job offers there are a number of internal hoops to

jump through, people will go out of their way for you if they like you. I would go as a far as to say likability is even more important than presenting a well-structured argument.

2. **Help them to understand why you are requesting what you are requesting** – it sounds obvious but it's easily forgotten, give them a reason, give them your why. This will help them to tell the story internally within the company and make the case as to why your request is justified. Remember you are not only trying to impress them, you are also looking to make it easy for them to overcome red tape, and by arming them with a well-thought-out reason you will make it easier for them to skip over these hurdles effortlessly.

3. **Understand their constraints** – Figure out where they are flexible and where they are not flexible. This skill enables you to find out the interests in which you can trade.

4. **You should care about the value of the entire deal, not the individual elements** – Deepak says by considering the deal as the whole package 'it gives them the flexibility of rewarding you in many different ways'. We've spoken about this at length. The key goal here is to look at everything that's on the table and use your 'Ideal, Acceptable and No go' table to map out what's really being proposed.

5. **They need to believe that they can get you** – 'nobody wants to be the stalking horse for the other the job'. If you are unobtainable, it could put them off going in to bat for you. A careful balance is required between presenting yourself as in demand and coming across as out of reach. They need to believe that given the right package they can secure you. It takes a lot of effort, time and influencing for the business to put a tailored package together. So

when they go to this effort, they want to know that you'll say yes.

6. **Don't negotiate just to negotiate** – this is very true, be careful not to negotiate for the sake of it, or because you think it's 'the done thing'. Instead, negotiate when something is important to you and highlight your order of preference on the things you are negotiating for. That way, you empower them to give you an attractive deal.

7. **Nothing is fundamentally more important than understanding the person on the other side of the table from you** – if you can do this, then you'll have the keys to the kingdom. This relates back to Dale Carnegie's words in *How to win friends and influence people*. People don't care about you, they care about them. When approaching a company for a job, you need to find out everything you can about them, the way it handles itself, what it values. Go for lunches, coffees, call up old colleagues. Do whatever it takes to find out as much as you can about the company.

8. **Negotiate multiple issues simultaneously** – this is about process. Don't say, 'The salary is kind of low, can you do something about it?' and then come right back at them with the next issue once they've sorted it, by stating 'a health insurance package would be nice'. Tackling one issue at a time is bound to annoy them and it's not effective. Instead, get all your negotiation points on the table upfront at the beginning. Highlight your preferences and the order of priority, that way you will give them the opportunity to go and secure it in one hit.

9. **Remember that what is not negotiable today, is maybe negotiable tomorrow** – as top negotiators we know that no doesn't always mean no. What it can mean is 'no, the way I see the world today'. The great thing about this is, things change. Budgets,

people, strategies, companies and objectives, all shift over time, therefore in 6 months you may be in a position to have a different conversation from the one you are having today.

10. **Stay at the table** - stay in touch, you never know when their constraints change. When you can learn more, stay at the table, get more information, don't just negotiate when it's time to negotiate.

11. **Be prepared for tough questions** - know what you are going to say if they ask you, 'Do you have any other interviews currently?' and respond in a truthful, yet professional way. To do this, think about what they might be interested in finding out from you.

12. **Focus on the intent of the question** - why are they asking you this question? What are they trying to find out?

13. **Avoid ultimatums** - don't make them feel like you're making ultimatums, e.g. I'll only take the job if the salary is above x.

14. **They're not out to get you** - these people like you, they have their own issues to deal with, they may be busy. Remember this and it will take you far.

15. **Understand the person you are negotiating with** - don't let one person in a company ruin your view of a company.

10

IT'S SHOW TIME
PART 2: BIG TICKET ITEMS

'Never let success get to your head,
never let failure get to your heart.'

HERE IS WHERE the rubber really meets the road. Big ticket items change the dynamic of the negotiation but not in the way you might imagine. It can sometimes be easier to negotiate when there is more money, increased time or a bigger commitment involved. Small ticket items can, in fact, matter more to a business or person because there is more at stake. In smaller negotiations there may be less margin and, therefore, decreased flexibility or the context of the situation my make the negotiation harder to navigate because offering you a discount or free access when they are just starting out in business may set a precedent they don't want to entertain. The thing with big ticket items is, on average we get less exposure to negotiating them and there can often be more outwardly spoken hype and external focus on us due to the fact that it's a large deal. In this chapter, I will break down some of the most common negotiation situations where the purchase or order is typically larger than normal. Just as with smaller negotiations, emotions have a way of creeping in here too, and depending on the context, they will leave your negotiation leverage in tatters. In maneuvering through all of this, I'd advise you to focus less on what a big deal it is and look at the opportunity for collaboration and to perfect your integrative negotiation style. After all, this is a sure-fire way to ensure that you get maximum value.

10.1 How to Negotiate When You Have a Large Order

When you have a larger than normal order or multiple orders, such as booking a venue five times throughout the year or you buying 60 laptops for your business, the situation calls for a step negotiation.

This refers to the process of starting the negotiation based on a volume of one or two products, services or hires and agreeing on the appropriate discount for that volume of business.

Once you have reached an agreement on the basis of this volume to you, you then step up again and say, 'OK, now how about if I were to buy five items.' The process is then repeated until you reach your desired order size. As you can see, you are stepping up the volume of products negotiated and, in turn, achieving greater rewards for bringing this level of business.

A step negotiation works well because it allows the seller to get excited at each step. Imagining the order size doubling, tripling each time or even more. This excitement translates into significantly better deals for you as the buyer.

Consider the alternative approach. If you call up and ask flat out what's the best deal they could do on 60 laptops, you're probably not going to get the best result.

Why?

Well, there are a number of reasons you might not achieve the best outcome based on an order of this size. Firstly, you spend less time building a rapport with the seller and so there is less emphasis on the order actually coming off. It's assumed that it will happen and, therefore, automatically it doesn't seem like such a big deal when you go to place the order. It's the basic reward principles of psychology playing out here; the step negotiations build up anticipation and positive emotion, and the thought process is rewarding. In contrast, large volume orders that appear out of the blue are exciting but can be perceived as being in the bag or unimportant if you ask for too much in return because the process of building up the order was not engaged in by the seller.

By engaging in a step negotiation, where the order size increases step by step, you naturally create a situation whereby further discounts or benefits are implied due to the increase in volume purchased. The seller is also excited by the potential to increase the order and will work harder to achieve these results. The step negotiation implies there is more to lose. As order volume can decrease as well as increase, it rests on the level of discount between steps and additional services to make the deal worthwhile for the buyer.

The best way to test it out is to call a different store of the same brand and check it out. In one case, ask them outright what they could do for the full order and in the other do a step negotiation. This way you'll see first-hand which presents the more appealing route.

Of course, you have an advantage when you have a larger order to place and if there are multiple sellers of that product you have an even bigger advantage. You can use the abundance of supply as a method of playing them off against each other, ensuring you get the best deal. A word of warning with this strategy, though. It must be done while keeping the self-esteem of the seller intact. If you plan on building a genuine and sustainable relationship with this seller, then you must present the fact that you have other options in a subtle but charming way. It's a bit like when you go on a date. When you like someone, you want to present yourself as in demand without coming across like you are just out for the best offer or arrogant and have multiple options.

Maintaining your integrity in the process is key to working through the step negotiation, as it is in any negotiation. Integrity and the way you conduct yourself through the deal and interact with others needs to remain consistent at all times.

When you have a larger than normal order to place it can go to your head and ruin the foundation of a fruitful relationship because of ego getting in the way. It's important to remember that a big volume doesn't automatically guarantee a big discount; there will have been bigger orders than yours in the past and there will be in the future; it's not a competition with others.

What it is, however, is an opportunity to take your book of business, loyalty and relationship with the seller to the next level. This is what the focus should be on, not comparisons with other buyers or past sales. This is your opportunity to create a unique deal built on the relationship that has been formed between the buyer and seller at this very moment in time.

10.2 Weddings, Engagements and Babies

Wow. In three words, I have just described a heck of a lot of money that could potentially be spent in a relatively short amount of time. With all three things – babies, engagements and weddings – emotions play a big part. So by getting the right people and being clear and upfront, you will save you both time and a small fortune.

This is also a great opportunity for you to practise your negotiation skills. Just the word 'wedding' seems to increase prices by 50%-100%; remember, these guys do this every day and they know how to make a profitable business out of your emotions. Now I am not saying that wedding planners, jewellers and baby stores don't provide necessary and valuable services, they absolutely do. What I want you to think about is the relationship, so find a wedding planner that will work with you, get you the most for your money and level with you. You need to be able to speak openly and honestly to these folks. People get carried away and get into debt as a result of weddings, engagements and babies because they get sucked in and the sales people are very, very good. When you experience exceptional sales you will feel it. You won't quite know what has happened other than the fact that you walked into the store two hours ago and now your arms are full, struggling to balance the latest stroller, new cot and any number of things you didn't plan to get. You'll feel happy and your credit card will feel lighter. These are the three realms where exceptional sales professionals live and you are walking into their den because, you guessed it, your emotions are front and centre in each of these topics.

To counter this, you will need discipline to set boundaries and deadlines that you, as a couple, agree on and will stick to.

Weddings

My advice for weddings is to get a budget that's realistic and you can afford (e.g. you have the money to pay for it in the bank account ready to go, or at least have monthly direct debits set up to transfer a set amount each month to the wedding fund to ensure you save the appropriate amount each month).

For example, consider this; the wedding is in 20 months' time and it's going to cost roughly $12,000. This means you will need to put away (12k/20) $600 a month to make the budget.

Then, go to the wedding planner, say you have a budget of $10k for the wedding and make your requests.

If problems and disagreements about prices arise at this stage, then this is probably not the wedding planner for you. What you want here is a situation where you end up spending a little more than your $10k budget, but for that extra $2k you get a whole lot more thrown in. You want the wedding planners to try to get you up, and for you coming up they throw in incentives to make it more appetising. Capish.

The other option is to organise the wedding yourself. This means you have the opportunity to negotiate with a wider range of different parties from florists to musicians. That could be fun! If you have the time, then the way to get a better deal is to focus on getting to know each supplier. The more they can get to know you as a couple and the more that they like you, the more likely it is you will get a deal that's tailored to your needs.

This is all to do with connections as well. We know that friends and family are a big help when it comes to pulling off a wedding, but don't forget about making new connections. Don't be afraid to cold call and put it on the table. Always wanted your fairy-tale wedding in a dream castle? Call up some castles and see what they can do. For the right person, anything is possible. Food and drink carry the bulk of the expense at weddings. Get that right and you're on to a winner. Call local breweries, caterers; anything you can do to get mates' rates on these two will go a long way to reducing the overall bill.

Getting married abroad? Boy, you're in for a treat. Having been there and done that, it comes down to the people. You need to find someone to work on your behalf and leverage their buying power (e.g. the fact that they do a number of weddings per year for their suppliers and can, therefore, negotiate better rates on food and drinks). Renting out a villa? Check out whether they will charge you for having the ceremony there. The word wedding means multiple and so you want to avoid using it too much. A wedding negotiation is an opportunity to get creative, and there are a multitude of considerations and variables that can all be tweaked to offer more value. Unless you've got the world-famous Franck from *Father of the Bride* planning your wedding, then there will be the opportunity to roll up your sleeves and get negotiating. Food and beverages along with venue hire are typically the big-ticket items; therefore, any percentage discounts you can agree here will have a dramatic effect on the overall bill.

Think about it from the supplier's point of view. They deal with weddings, brides, grooms, planners all day, every day, and are just waiting for the question 'can you do a discount'. And guess what, they will have their response prepared down to a tee. Enjoy this moment as you will observe a highly articulate and well thought out rebuttal. Don't be surprised by this, expect it. This is what they do for a living.

It's also them protecting their margins. At some price points, it doesn't become worth it to the seller to take the wedding on. So by knowing this, and knowing they are prepared for our requests by having decent answers to shoot us down, how do we approach it?

The way to go about this is to work with suppliers in a diagnostic manner. You are selling to the seller that you and your partner's wedding is different, different to all the weddings that have been before, and by doing this you move the needle away from the stock standard response and into the mutual respect zone. Here you are able to have a conversation that is different from the rest. By focusing on authenticity and the craft that they do, working with them to understand what is required, understanding their business and getting to know them as people, you will form a bridge into a new world where they see you as different to the others that have gone before.

Your requests will stand a better chance of not falling on deaf ears, as you have a seat at the table and you speak their language. You understand their challenges and together you are building a day that exists on mutual respect. Remember people like this are craftsmen and women; they love to create and now you can create together.

Engagement rings

This is a tricky one; they have you well and truly cornered here. They know that you know, that they know, that you need them. Let the mind games begin. Not only do you have your beautiful bride to be, the love of your life, to think of when you are shopping for this lifelong purchase, you also know that it will sit on her hand every day, professing your love to the world. So it will be judged by family and friends, passers-by, dogs, children and practically everyone that you will meet until you die. We know it's a big deal and we know that we need to get it right. But that doesn't mean you can't get a deal, even with all that pressure from a seller that sees you coming a mile off.

The first strategy is to get inspiration at the high-end expensive jewellers and then get the ring made up elsewhere. The second strategy is to source and negotiate the diamond separately from a diamond hub, like Hong Kong, where quality diamonds are often available at a discount.

The third strategy for engagement ring procurement is to shop around and play one store off against another. Prices tend to increase in an exponential fashion, but people vary massively in this field. This is where we will find our deal. Price is influenced by people, and people are the flexibility driver in this scenario.

We should at all times be conscious that this breed are experts in their trade. They are exceptional salespeople and know exactly how to position their pitch so that it doesn't even feel like one. It feels, instead, like you should be astounded that you managed to get so far without this diamond in your life and why haven't you come sooner.

Be warned, there's champagne and service, as well as sir and madaming as soon as you set foot through the door and into their world. This is their turf and they know it. They also know you; they are experts in people and will have you pegged within 30 seconds.

The best approach is to take charge by being informed. It's much better when you have an idea of what you want from the design, the look and feel of the ring, and the specifications. The most important are the four Cs: Cut, Carat, Clarity and Colour. These are the four elements of diamond grading that you will become very familiar with. Going up or down in one dimension rapidly changes the price and the quality. Make changes to the clarity and you will go up in price very sharply. The other thing to note is that the carat of the diamond doesn't always relate to size. You can have a smaller carat diamond that is only a fraction of a millimetre different in diameter (or the part that everyone will be looking at) but it will cost you thousands of dollars less.

Once the pleasantries are out of the way, the first question they'll ask is, do you know what you're looking for? In other words, how long have you been at this and am I your first stop on the list? If I am, then let me educate you on the trade and I can mould you into thinking my way. If not, I'll be more cautious and take my time to get to know you. If you know what you want and can speak their language, you are automatically in a stronger position.

Second question, do you have a budget in mind?

Put simply, this means what should I show you that is going to float your boat and make you fall in love. Where in the price range should I focus my efforts?

In this situation, it's best to be up front and approach the conversation as follows:

'Ideally my budget is between $10k-$12k'. Giving a range is good because you want them to show the more expensive rings as well and not just stick at the $10k end of the scale. By starting with a range, rather than a solid figure, you subtly create the air of possibility. That you may purchase at the higher end of your scale.

For example, say your actual budget is $10k-$10.5k, what you are aiming for is for the jeweller to give you a $12k ring for as close to $10k as possible.

If you just state $10k from the get go, then it's going to look suspect when you later say, 'Oh, now my budget is $12k, can you please show me those rings', and then when they do, you start requesting that they give it to you for $10k. The set up in the way the process unfolds is wrong and it's unlikely it will happen. It simply looks too obvious.

After they have given you a quote for a variety of engagement rings to your liking and you get a feel for what your money gets you, I'd be quite frank with them and say, 'To be honest, I am going to go to whoever can give me the biggest discount, we have a lot of other costs coming up and this is just one item on the list.'

Then say, 'I really like this $12k one, but I'd need the price to be closer to $10k. Can you see what you can do on price please?' Then they'll go away, do some calculations based on the US Dollar exchange rates and their margins. They will essentially be looking at their sales book and how much they need the sale in terms of revenue versus profit margin.

When weighing up the pros and cons, is it better for them to make a reduced margin but get the sale and a customer who they can sell insurance for the ring to, and then the pair of wedding rings as well? Or is it more important to them that you don't go to a competitor? Do you have friends that are likely to be getting married and will you recommend them when people compliment the ring?

Don't underestimate the power you have in this situation. Word of mouth and personal referrals will make a massive difference in this type of crowded industry. If you like your friend's engagement ring, you are going to go check out the store when your turn comes around. All this plays into the evaluation and mindset of the seller.

When they come back, they'll say a price that's not $10k but maybe $11k or slightly under like $10.8k.

That's fine and good because you are establishing a relationship, which is important to do. I should also point out that jewellers and sellers expect you to negotiate. They do it day in day out so they are very good at it and control most of the variables, but not all of them.

It will depend on factors, such as the exchange rate to US Dollar, the number of sales they've had that month, if they like you and who they are as a person and how you come across as a person or couple.

When they say $10.8k, just reply, 'OK, thanks for looking into that, I really need to be at $10k or closer to make it work. I've got a whole day to get this sorted so I am going to check out the other stores as well.' You should have already conducted a thorough check of all the other stores if you have got to this point in order to establish your BATNA. The store you are currently in should be the target store where you want to buy a ring from.

Here you have a choice:

- If you think the seller wants a sale and could be up for doing a deal right then and there, and you are comfortable with this and know you have found the ring you want, then go for it. Be straight with them and say, 'I do like the ring but the most I can do is $10.2k, if we can make it work at that, then I'll get it right now.' Not only will this counter offer work, because it creates a sense of urgency, but it will also show that you have made a decision and price is the final barrier.

- If they don't look like they'll do a deal, ask them to write down the details of the ring and go have some lunch somewhere. Make sure they make a note of the ring you like on their system and they are able to find it again for you easily. The absolutely worst-case scenario would be if you went to all this trouble to find your ideal ring and then the jeweller would not be able to locate the exact same ring which you had your heart set on. I speak from experience when I say this can happen, no matter how professional the outfit. At the end of the day, some sales people will tell you it is the ring that you saw when you go back, even when there's a possibility that it might not be. Not because they are lying but because of human error, mistakes are made. If possible, take a photo. Some outfits won't let you do this for fear of replication elsewhere, but if you're a serious buyer and you use your powers of charm and persuasion, explaining that you don't want to lose the ring, then they just might let you. This is just one way of safeguarding and protecting your hard work. Now with the ring located, the ball is in your court. You can call them up the next day and negotiate over the phone rather than going back in. That way you have increased power again. When you are in front of them, sipping away on champagne, relaxing in luxurious chairs, eyes scanning the array of fine jewels bestowed upon you, they have a front row seat to all of your reactions, and by virtue of you being in their shop, on their turf, they have more control over the situation. When you are on the phone, you are further away and they don't know how many other jewellers you are talking to. Time has passed and you are asking for a sale with them, all they need to do is say yes. If they say no, then you can go back and try again in person this time and appeal to the relationship that you have built. Either way, you'll be in a winning position because they've already given you the $10.8k and they will most likely knock off a few more dollars to get the deal over the line. Being so close to the finish line, it doesn't make sense for most sales houses (if they've set their business up correctly) not to do the deal for the sake of a few hundred dollars. The extra new business you could bring them, plus the brand marketing you'll do for free, is worth it. The engagement ring game is a buyer's economy, dressed up in sellers' clothing. At first glance, it feels like the sellers have all the power in the equation, but when you strip it back you will find that you the buyer can wield a great deal of influence in the negotiation and engineer a fair and equitable deal.

- How much is your insurance on the ring? Jewellers also sell ring insurance, which you'll most likely need anyway, so use this as a final bargaining chip. I can do $10.2 and if you can make that happen, I'll also purchase the insurance policy from you. Double win!

Engagement parties

Not as colossal as the engagement ring expense, but engagement parties still have the potential to leave a large dint in your bank balance and parties of this nature can blow out of all proportion if you are not careful. Like with a wedding, the venue, food and beverages are where the bulk of the costs are. A tip for getting an affordable venue is to use new ones or venues that haven't held engagement receptions before. Both will have a less established or incentivised fee structure. Why? Because they want publicity and the opportunity of new business.

What you want to avoid here is getting fixated on one must-have venue. If you do, then you fall into a standard pattern of negotiation and they may not even give you a discount if it's a popular venue because they're fully booked. You become a small player on a big machine.

By focusing your negotiation strategy on new businesses or venues that haven't thrown a party for an engagement before, you'll capture their energy and excitement to hold the event. See how the tables are turned; suddenly, they are the ones vying for your business rather than the other way around. Ultimately, they'll want to impress both on price and service, and will relish the opportunity to show off their special venue to 50 of your closest friends and family. It's excellent PR for them and exceedingly good for your bank balance as they'll likely end up doing a stonking deal on everything.

Babies

Now here's another one that has the potential to milk you dry. This is about being savvy as it comes down to pure street smarts. You will need to have your wits about you when going into a baby store or else you will come out six hours later, armed with more treasures than Jack Sparrow, not knowing what happened.

Practical intelligence is to be applied here. It's like the conveyer belt on Bruce Forsyth's *The Generation Game* inside these stores. As things come along, you pick them up and momentum builds. One thing leads to another and before you know it, you have a Sophie the Giraffe and Dora The Explorer backpack and you only went in to 'have a look'.

Babies are a huge market and the big companies have got it covered in an expensive, designer way. My advice is, if you want a Bugaboo, then get it and play on the fact that a lot of places sell them and use this to your advantage. It's quick-fire, one-shot negotiation in the world of babies; go in and ask to speak to a manager. Say, 'Right, we need to spend some money but I'm going to need to get some deals as well. What would you recommend to make that happen?' Put it back on to them. If they want your business, as opposed to you going into the other 1 million baby stores, then they need to hook you up with a deal.

Then get them to show you what they can do; let them sell. Build a rapport and make it fun. It doesn't need to take long and means that while you are going around collecting stuff in the shop, walking around letting your heartfelt emotions of love for your little prince or princess guide you, you are now back in control. This is about economies of scale, commerciality and mindset. I can spend in your shop or I can spend in the shop two minutes away, your choice. You've flipped the switch and you have them listening.

'Car seats, right this way, Sir.' You are more likely to get a deal when buying in bulk with baby stuff. It's just the way it works, so I suggest doing all your research online and in the stores. Then pick a day to do it all, which will be known as 'baby day'. Know what you want before you walk in. Find someone with authority to give you a sweet deal. Independent and smaller shops may have more capacity for this, as larger shops tend to stick by the rules unless they can offer display products at a reduced price. There is definitely flexibility to get a deal on show products, this will come down to timing.

Phone a friend; with babies it's handy to know someone in the industry as you can call in a favour and ask for a staff discount. As babies grow at a speed that means all the stuff you bought only three months ago is now redundant, the second-hand market for barely used baby stuff is also booming.

Cute baby discount

We recently welcomed our beautiful baby boy into the world, Levi Leonardo. He has been the best thing that has ever happened to us and we are truly over the moon. The excitement of having a baby and going through some tougher economic times in the Lopez Castle family has seen me more frequently asking for discounts in the fun of the moment.

The opportunity for discounts is really everywhere, as long as we ask for them. I've used everything from 'new dad discount' to getting a refund on a boxing gym payment that I wanted to get cancelled and 'cute baby discount' on something as simple as coffee.

The point here is that the opportunity for a discount is always possible; it just depends on what the motivation for giving it is. Being real and bringing people into your situation is what changes the dynamic here.

The truth is, we were hard up on cash after having a baby and I hadn't used the gym once (even though I would have loved to). Being honest about where you are and what's going on for you brings the other person into your world; the key is that you *ask* for what it is you want.

> To: tim.castle@live.co.uk
> Subject: Re: Please put gym membership on hold from today onwards
>
> Hi Tim,
>
> Congratulations about being a Father!
>
> Normally we don't refund unless we made a mistake but love to do for
> you.
>
> Please confirm your account detail for payment.
>
> Best regards, Fight Gym Manly
>
>
> On 06/10/2016 07:42, tim.castle@live.co.uk wrote:
> > Hi Fight Gym,
> >
> > Just seen it's taken the payment today, is there any possibility to
> > get a refund as since signing up I haven't actually used the gym once.
> > I just found out I'm going to be a father so could do with the cash if
> > possible?
> >
> > Best,
> > Tim

Then the other person has a choice; they can either step into your world and meet your request or they can choose to go a different route. Either way, you made the request and that's what matters. I'm not suggesting you use your baby as a bargaining chip to get deals through the door – well, depending on the situation ;) – but I am suggesting that you spot the opportunity and understand that deals are possible and easier than we sometimes think.

Most people in life aren't arseholes. They want to help and be part of the journey, and by sharing a bit of your world with them you can literally make their day as well as yours.

So the next time you're out and you come across a scenario where you think deals are possible, think 'cute baby discount'. Know that it's possible and then figure out how you can bring that person into your world.

10.3 Airlines

With airlines, it's about making the most of promotional sales and offers. As there's not a lot of fat in airline tickets, discounts are hard to come by. My recommendation is to get an American Express Explorer Card that will put yourself in a more favourable position as it has an introductory offer of 100,000 bonus points, which you can then use to turn them into air miles for your airline of choice (e.g. Singapore Airlines).

Cards, such as the AMEX, are good for getting a quick boost up the ladder in another domain, usually because they offer relatively high amounts of bonus points in exchange for a relatively low spend within the introductory period. Perfect if you are, say, buying an engagement ring, for instance.

Transfer these points across and get yourself up to Gold Status with the airline; this will then give you access to lounges, as well as helping with other requests. On every flight you take, be sure to ask the check-in desk if there is any chance of an upgrade to Business Class. You never know when this request will be obliged, especially when travelling long haul. It may not happen on leg one of the journey, but then on leg two you may miraculously get a nice surprise and be upgraded to Business Class.

When considering airlines, you want to be negotiating on the flight change fees, extra leg room seats, and if you have a baby, a location near to the toilets and bassinets, seats without another passenger next to you, and so on and so forth. Airline negotiations are about getting the perks that will make your journey as comfortable as possible, not the cash saving.

Consolidating your points in this way will do you a favour as loyalty is everything in the airline world. And so it should be; loyalty is an excellent attribute and when the service is enjoyable, it works both ways.

More generally, being street smart and knowing when not to give up or when to ask the awkward questions, is a matter of experience. We live in a world where we are constantly told by society through the media, culture and our interpersonal relationships how we should behave. Having the guts to ask for an upgrade is just common sense, but when the world tells us it's not 'the done thing' or is 'never going to happen' we get cold feet and don't ask, meaning we fail to maximise the opportunity. It's really simple; pick the check-in person that looks like they are having a good day, then ask outright, 'I don't suppose there's the chance of a free upgrade to business on the flight today?' Smile, pause and make light of the fact that you just asked. Don't sweat it, it's just a question. Whatever their reaction is, that's on them, not you.

10.4 Cars

We've all been warned about the crafty car salesmen who sells you the bargain of a lifetime that three weeks later turns out to be no better than your grandma's washing machine, as it's constantly breaking down and is louder than a tractor. Not all of these cunning creatures are bad or dodgy, but you need to take you're 'A-game' to this one, especially if you are buying a second-hand motor. The new car market is less fun, so we'll leave that one as it's already set up in favour of the buyer. The second-hand car market, however, is where the opportunities are.

When negotiating you have a wealth of opportunities and comparison points up your sleeve, ranging from Gumtree, to enthusiastic friends and family, to getting the car checked out by your mechanic. In this situation, it comes down to getting an expert opinion. Don't be afraid to take charge here and make it clear from the beginning that the only way a sale will be going through is after the green light from your garage.

On price, go in at 30%-35% lower than the advertised one and see where you get to, then work back from there. They may laugh, berate you or look as if you've come from Mars; this is good, as it shows you who you are dealing with. If they carefully explain that this is not possible and suggest a more suitable price (and you'll know what a good deal, OK deal and rip-off is because you will have done your homework), then you will see you are interacting with someone more likely to build a stable relationship.

If they laugh at you, make you feel uncomfortable or walk away in disgust, then you know who you're dealing with too. Do you really want to pick up the phone to this person in three weeks' time, asking why the car has fallen to pieces? With cars, above all else, trust your gut. What you want is someone who is reasonable with whom you get along. The world has enough problems without adding untrustworthy car salesmen into the mix. Making a profit is not the issue; they're a business and that's fine. What you are looking for are qualities of high character.

It's like speed dating to find the right match, aim for someone you can have a laugh with and you'll find the right car at the right price.

10.5 Telecoms, Internet and TV

If a service is shoddy, call them up and ask them for a refund on previously paid for services. Internet slower than advertised? It's worth a phone call to see what they can do.

At the end of your phone contract, your service provider will be bending over backwards to keep you as their customer. It is when they are at their most vulnerable; hence, they'll give you more love at this stage. So make your requests and see what they say. There's plenty of good deals out there for phones and the competition is only going to increase as we become a more connected world. This is most definitely a buyer's market and markets, such as telecoms where there isn't a monopoly, give you a leg up.

If the charges don't look right, or you get higher than average bills, don't just accept it. Call them up and talk it through with them. There's always a retrospective price reduction or removal of fees that can be done if you ask politely. These companies play on the fact that most people won't even bother to call up to dispute the fees and so they're making pure profit on the basis of penalty charges or automatic charges for reaching a data limit without warning.

Currently in 2017, you can have some of the most fun and low value negotiations to start building up your negotiation muscle. Need to get out of your phone contract asap? Call them up and negotiate the exit without any extra charges. It can be done and it is excellent practice for future higher stakes negotiations.

When I was starting out learning to negotiate I would, and still do, call when there's an issue with a bill, product or service. I can't think of a single time when I didn't receive a refund or credit into my account because of having a chat. I encourage you to practise on these negotiations that don't matter so much in the grand scheme of things. I used to negotiate on behalf of friends as a way of racking up experience, and once I started getting results, the tables turned and people started calling me to negotiate on their behalf.

Phone, internet and TV contracts are the big ones because situations change at lightning speed in this fast-paced world. People break up, jobs are lost, jobs are won, people move countries; ultimately, our plans change and the small print in contracts that we never have time to read suddenly becomes important when we're trying to get out of a lease or a service.

To overcome this, call and keep calling until you find someone who relates to your situation. When you find a person who gets what you are going through and has perhaps even been in your shoes, they will help you to share information and use their influence internally within the organisation, easing open the doors to success. It's often when we are most beaten down that other things happen to beat us down further. Yet the world is filled with good-spirited people who are willing to help. It's a numbers game; you just have to find them and then work with them to make your situation better. Sometimes, it's on the first call; sometimes, it's on the 100th.

Fundamentally, when negotiating on big ticket items, your ability to deal with people plays a huge part in the framing, bargaining and outcome of your negotiation. To wrap up this heavy hitting chapter on big deals, which have the potential to either break the bank or give you a mighty pleasant saving, I want to leave you with one final point.

Keep in mind at all times how you are framing your nego-tiations and constantly ask yourself, are you approaching the negotiation from what you need or what they need? By checking in with yourself and answering this very simple question, you will be able to chart the course to successful negotiation. The more you can discover about their motivations, and get the other side talking about what matters to them, the more you are actually paying them a compliment. And who doesn't love a compliment. Complimenting them, makes them feel important. Everyone loves to be made to feel important. It's a law of human nature. Be sure to be genuine though, flattery will get you nowhere, genuine interest with a solution-focused mindset will pay dividends. To ensure you have more success in your negotiations on big ticket items indulge this philosophy. It's much more possible than you might think to get some fantastic deals if you follow these rules.

11

MAKE IT HAPPEN

'You didn't wake up today to be mediocre.
Don't wait for opportunity, create it.'

YOU ARE NOW on the home straight. You've gone through the basics of negotiation and preparation, you understand what to look out for in terms of body language and you've mastered a range of various negotiation success strategies for specific scenarios. As I said earlier on, my motto is: 'There's a negotiation everyone,' and you my friend, now have the skills to be a top negotiator, enabling you to create value, inspire others and maximise your meaningful relationships to make a difference today. Don't let anything or anyone hold you back or tell you different – not your mindset, our parents or your boss. Go at it each and every day with fresh eyes, learning all the time, and implement the lessons as you progress. Make as many mistakes as you can, be bold and stand right back up again, for each day that we strive to rise above mediocre is a day that takes us closer to our vision. Mediocrity kills creativity and that my friend is not you. You are oozing with options, looking for alternative ways of doing things, hungry to take on and absorb new perspectives. This is your time to shine.

11.1 Take Action

Negotiation isn't only about knowing when to say the right thing; it's also about taking action to get ahead of the game. You can't just rest on your laurels when there's business to be done, doors that can be opened and a process that can be fast-tracked.

Say, for instance, you're having some money issues. You've gone and maxed out your credit card to pay for some medical expenses. Actually, let's take it a step further; you've gone and maxed out your credit card bills by taking out hard, cold cash, meaning you're likely to be getting charged the highest rate of interest, and you have more expenses coming up that are going to require even more credit. To make matters more complex, you're also living in a foreign country and your visa expires in four months meaning that your local bank won't help you out of this mess with a loan with a decent rate of interest because you are considered a risk.

What do you do?

Every day you sit with the balance on that card, it's charging you at 21.59% per annum; it's like you can't move. Plugging into your search engine reveals plenty of 0% balance transfer cards that are available; only not for you, due to your circumstances. You've only got four months left remember; even though you're not planning on leaving the country and will be getting your visa renewed when it runs out, in the eyes of the bank you are a flight risk.

The way to solve this sticky situation is to get human and get into action mode.

Step 1. Work out between your pay cheque, assets for sale, stocks, tax rebates, bonuses that you can pay off in the next month and what's remaining. This is your figure.

Step 2. Look online; yes persistence is key, but that's not everything

Step 3. Start applying – get rejected, call them up, find out why. See if they'll reopen it, based on your conversation.

Step 4. Look for the bank that doesn't ask for passport or ID verification in its initial assessment process. It comes down to searching for the part of the process that is blocking you access to what you want.

Step 5. Apply for this balance transfer credit card.

Step 6. Immediately after you have applied, pick up the phone and call them. Don't even make a cup of tea; get straight into action. Have your last two pay slips handy on email, ready to send.

Say this: 'Hi, I have just applied for the balance transfer credit card and wanted to check that everything was OK with the application. Could you check for me please, I have the reference number.'

'Yes, certainly Sir/Madam,' will be their response Be polite, calm and attentive; give the phone your full attention.

Step 7. All we need is to verify your income, they will say. Jump in and say, 'I have my pay slips right here. I can send them to you'. Don't let them pass you off; get an email address out of them to send them to. It's important; this person is going to help approve your application.

Step 8. Ask for their name. Send them over and wait for them to do their checking.

Step 9. Get approved.

Notice the winning ingredient in this cycle to solving this problem was getting ahead of it before they could reject you on whatever grounds don't fit their typical process. By speaking to them on the phone, you humanise the situation. By behaving calmly, you are professional and this helps to convey your story with conviction. These are perceptions that can't be presented online, where you are just a number, and you fit into a queue and formalised process. You need to become a face; you need to become real but not pushy.

If you liked that one, try this next one on for size. Say that you're ill and waiting for some important test results. You go to the doctor, get checked out and they send a sample off to the lab. Ask your doctor who they are sending them to and find out the name. Next day, call up the lab and ask to speak directly to that person. You'll find that if you ask confidently and clearly, they'll put you right through. Remember, it's all in your head; only you think you're not meant to be ringing up. That's the doctor's job. They speak to the doctor if anything is up and so the process goes around. Sometimes the rules don't apply. When you need answers for your family, you gotta do what you gotta do.

My point here is that you've got to act. You've got to make the calls. Spend the time getting the information out of people. It's called hustling and the better you get at opening doors and making the wheels turn, the better your negotiations will be. Why? Because each time you open a door or make the process go a little faster than it normally does, you are negotiating and are getting a better quality of life as a result.

In both examples (and they're real by the way) you are getting access to richer information and you can control the stages of what happens next. What does the lab recommend? Why is your application being denied? What options do you have?

Negotiation is about creating options for yourself. That is one of the results. The process is done by getting up and out into the world and talking to the decision-makers before the virtual systems and online software can decide your fate.

Being a hustler is fun. It takes massive amounts of grit and once you get into the rhythm of it, it's surprisingly easy. Like a snowball rolling down the side of a mountain, it slowly gathers pace, and as it does so, it takes on more snow as it goes, getting bigger and forging its own path.

This ain't Kansas, Dorothy. You need to make it happen; take control of the rudder and steer that ship all the way to the port. Just because someone tells you no, doesn't mean it's a no! It just means keep going.

11.2 Go for it

There's a point in every negotiation when you need to go for it. You need to be bold and take the negotiation in the direction you want it to go. Successful negotiations don't just get a successful outcome by having all the ingredients; you need to know how to skilfully blend them together to create a masterpiece.

Imagine you are baking a cake and you've mixed all the ingredients together and it's now time to put the cake in the oven and see it rise. This is the point in the negotiation where you need to boldly state what you want.

By being bold, I don't mean shouting, demanding or being loud; what I'm referring to is courage. Having the courage to push forward to express what you need and to know how to do it. If you only go in with half the effort, then you can only expect half the results.

The other day I had a very quick negotiation. I needed to get a refund on a shirt in a shop that didn't do refunds. I walked confidently back into the shop; instantly the two sales assistants recognised me and as if by magic, right on cue asked me, 'How was the shirt?'

I smiled and replied, 'The shirt is good but I need to return it,' as I marched over towards the counter. The first sales assistant joined me at the front counter and asked if I wanted to exchange it for anything else (holding her cards close, upselling). I said no, I just needed a refund, to which she replied, 'We don't do refunds (revealing her cards).' So far, it had been a pretty standard discussion and to the point, as expected.

What I did next was the difference between refund or no refund and buying some clothes I didn't want. I said, 'What, you don't do refunds?' exclaiming my surprise. 'Yeah, we don't do refunds,' she replied, 'if you wanted a refund, you need to shop at Myer or David Jones.' This is a red herring, don't get caught up in this. It is a distraction, meant to throw you off the scent and also set a boundary or benchmark as is the standard practice. I said, 'I don't want to exchange for anything else, I came in because I liked that shirt but I don't suit the fit.'

I then pushed forward. This was the time to go for it and deliver what I wanted. I said, 'Will you, on this occasion, refund this shirt considering I only purchased it the other night and it's unworn. I mean, I was here under 24 hours ago.' So, I didn't get caught up in the alternative discussion and pointed out that this shirt was the only reason I was in the shop, and then reflected back on the current situation, that I'd purchased the shirt less than 24 hours ago and it was unworn. This highlighted the reality of the situation and indicated an easy resale; unblocking the path from focusing on protocol and what's 'normal' practice in this market to instead focus on the reality that all she needed to do was refund me for a shirt that I was choosing to return because it doesn't suit me. It wasn't not because I don't like it; I wanted it to work but it just didn't suit me.

Then it came to down to her, as it always did, but rather than reverting to policy, we had now established an environment where if she said no it would be more difficult. The key is to deliver what you want in a clear and confident one liner; don't waffle, be confident and don't overcomplicate it or play the victim card. Just state the facts all the time in a warm and friendly manner. 'OK, only on this occasion,' she replied.

On a bigger scale and the same principles apply in business. Work out when to go for it, what's a distraction (red herring) and what to leave. If I had focused the conversation on the 'red herring', other stores that did refunds, and the differences between those stores and this store, it would have only strengthened both her argument and position.

Why?

Because by indulging this comment, I am acknowledging that there is a difference and by doing this I am making it easier for her to either hide behind or the reiterate the policy of the store. By focusing on our personal exchange, the specifics of this situation and the ease with which it could be done (the fact that the shirt hadn't been worn) made it easier to imagine a refund was possible.

This is what you need to do, be clear about what you want. If I had gone into the store, looked around a bit, then gone over to counter and asked for a refund it would have been a no. Why? Because the focus would have shifted to them trying to sell me something else in exchange because by walking around and looking I had suggested the possibility that there might be something else in the store I might want. That wouldn't support the argument that I only liked this shirt in the whole store and the negotiation would be over before it even had a chance to get going.

A lot of what happens in the 'go' phase of negotiation is determined by the actions that you take beforehand. Because I walked in, engaged in conversation, clearly stating why I was back, and walked directly over to the counter, all the signs indicated that I had one specific purpose. There was no opportunity for options involving exchange. Possibility has a lot to do with it and we must be careful that our pre- and post-actions don't reflect a possibility that takes away from our intended goal. Framing a situation and avoiding red herrings is also part of the skill.

When it's really time to go for it, you must hustle. There is only one way and that's forward. If you dilly-dally, it will only strengthen the other person's position. Pushing for answers at the right time is crucial and it can move the conversation into a place of new territory.

Picking the moment to 'go for it' is more of a sense than an exact timing. In some negotiations, like in the above example, it will come seconds into the value exchange. In others, it may be a second or third meeting before the opportunity arises.

One important thing is to make sure, as much as you can, that when you go for it you aren't going to be interrupted. A phone ringing or a staff member interrupting you are distracting and take away from the conversation at hand. It is important that you try to time it as best as possible to mitigate these types of distractions. Of course, we can't plan for everything and that's not what you want to do as it will come across as unauthentic, but choose a moment, as much as possible, when you think the other person is engaged and won't get distracted.

This is your final straight; you've done an 800-metre race and you've turned the final corner and you're 50 metres away from the finish line. You don't want the crowd to turn the other way because of a distraction just as you deliver the punchline. Think of it as if you're telling a story and it hinges on one sentence. This one sentence is about delivering possibility. To do that you must have a captive audience who's available to listen. Distraction damages this. The more you practice, the more your gut instinct will tell you when it's the right time. You will learn to gauge the situation intuitively and read the signals.

It is also important not to shy away from asking for what you want and delivering the one liner naturally and comfortably when the opportunity presents itself. There have been a number of occasions when I have spotted the opportunity to go for it; however, because I have not had all the facts or had the right conversations with management previously, I have had to let it pass by because I didn't know 100% what the business or my bosses wanted. This undoubtedly changes the course of the negotiation and it can be hard to get it back to create an opportunity again, so my advice for business negotiations is to seek the information you need so that you can perform when required.

That's why negotiations for things in your personal life are much easier, as you don't have to ask many other people for their views or requirements; you just have to ask yourself and be clear on what you want. In business, however, there are multiple stakeholders and multiple interests influencing what is wanted from a negotiation, and so it can be much harder to get answers before the opportunity to go for it presents itself.

My suggestion for business is, make sure you have a good crack at getting a feel for what management want as part of the preparation. When you have this, you can go full steam ahead.

Treat this phase of the negotiation as your own mini-business; people get up every day to train or work on their blogs and Instagram content; this is the same. As a negotiator, you are building a skill as part of your brand. Just as other people go out and take photos to build their brand on Instagram and take 50 shots to get the right one, you should treat practising negotiation in the same way.

11.3 Mastery

Highly ambitious people break their goals down into small steps and then align themselves with achieving these small steps really well. Over time, all of these small steps add up into the one big step, and what once looked impossible has been achieved. This then reinforces the behaviour that, in turn, becomes easier. That's how mastery is achieved: practice and reinforcement.

Mastery is achieved when you reach the unconscious competence stage and the skill becomes intuition (i.e. it's second nature and you can perform it without thinking about it consciously), according to the Four Stages of Competence, which was put forward by Noel Burch and developed by Gordon Training International. This is where you unconsciously ooze skill without thinking about what you're doing; you just do it and you love it. When you tap into your own life stream, you've got your groove. You love life and the doors just keep on opening. To progress through the four stages of competence and onwards to mastery, you need to practise, practise, practise, and your performance will improve over time due to your growing experience.

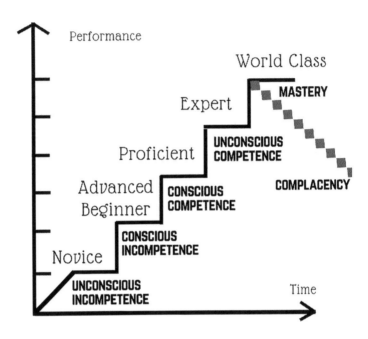

The thing I want you to take away from this book is that negotiation, as serious as it sounds, is just a way of getting the life that you want. It enables you to roll with the rhythm of life and get the most out of it. I truly believe that people who don't tap into this life source only scrape the surface of their own potential. Feel that fire burning inside; that's where you dig deep. It's where you back yourself and get the biggest inspiration, the motivation and your passion and zest for life.

People say you need to think of it like this: 'What's the worst that can happen?' That's correct, but only from a liberation point of view. If you are relying on that type of motivation to explain why you ask for a deal or try to get what you want, it's not enough. It's great for getting over the fear of asking, but it's also framed in a way that the answer to 'What's the worst that can happen?' is 'They say no.' It's like you're accepting no before you even begin.

Now, I'm not saying that 'no' won't be their response or the appropriate response. What I am saying is it goes deeper than that when you truly negotiate. When you truly want it, you don't need to liberate yourself and then force yourself to act, as you're acting from a different part. You're tapping into the very part of you that makes you, you, and you're acting from that part. You're living.

I am sat in a hotel lobby in Sweden right now. It's 4am. I was lying here in a comfy bed and I just had to get up and write this. Each chapter has been written when I have been at my most inspired. I wanted this book to be real. To be made up of insights when I felt them. A manual to transform the way that you negotiate and live life.

Take what you want from it and leave the rest. I'm not saying that it will work for everyone in the same way, but I hope that you will find some value in it. Simply relying on what's the worst that can happen is only the tip; it's not enough.

11.4 Commitment Case Study

Michael Jordan

An example is Michael Jordan. He was left out of the varsity basketball team in his sophomore year, and from that moment on he made a commitment to practice daily and train harder than ever before. That commitment to himself, that belief in his talent gave him the courage and confidence to keep going. It's the same with negotiation. It's the same principle of training hard, putting in the hours of practice that are going to elevate you to new levels of success and move you through the four stages of competence.

Michael Jordan's Lesson:

1. **When in doubt, train harder** – experience is what takes you from A to B and then on to Z. The road to becoming a top negotiator stems from daily practice in the real world.

11.5 Put it All on the Line

There have been a few key times when I have put it on the line to create the situation where I needed to make it happen.

One was when I quit my job in Australia. I was on a business visa that meant when you quit, you only had 90 days to find a new job to sponsor you or you were out.

I knew I needed to do something different, a new challenge, but I also knew that unless I put myself in the position where I needed to make it happen, I wouldn't be motivated enough to really push and find it. I went out and I found it; there was no other road. I put myself in that position.

Now, I'm not saying quit your job if you want more. Hmmm actually, I am. Sometimes, we need to put ourselves in the position to find the motivation, to tap into that life source to find the real you. To stop procrastinating, to stop listening to our fears and doubts.

I've done this several times in my life. I wanted to travel to Australia, but deep down I was worried. Worried about taking a year out of college; how would I find the money?

I wanted to move to London. As I've already mentioned previously, transitioning out of university for the second time wasn't easy. But it was the direction I needed to take to make it happen, to get my life going where it needed to go. Sometimes, all we need to do is act instead of waiting, and trust that we will find ourselves and the grit to make it happen.

In effect, we are creating a 'what's the worst that can happen situation', but instead of saying this to motivate ourselves, we are actually doing it. This is different because when you create a situation where you dramatically change your life and circumstances, you are forced to live closer to the edge. You create the opportunity for a fire that's burning deep inside to come out.

My advice is this: if you are really pushing for that pay rise and don't get it, leave. If you are worth what you think you are, then you'll find someone who will value you elsewhere and who will be in sync with you.

If you want to travel but are too scared, get a friend and negotiate the situation until it makes sense to you.

Risk and fear hold us back. We are programmed to fear the unknown and uncertainty deceptively blocks our path. But when we confront the problem head on, we start to make progress and the fog lifts.

Turning 'no' into 'yes' is easier when it's all on the line; you push yourself harder. You believe more. You get closer to you.

A word of caution; when you do this, make sure you have wholesome people around you. Don't make a bold life move and then run back to the naysayers. Keep your cards close and maintain momentum. You need positive people around you. As Ray Dailo says, you need to triangulate with more discerning people, meaning only allow those with good judgement into your circle.

Comfort zones, they are a big one. You are so capable; you just have to tap into that life stream and being busy is an excellent way to do this.

I went through a rut for about five years, nothing much apart from travel and nights out was exciting to me. I was living for these moments but not for a full life. Living for the ups, but not really tapping into the in between times.

Now I live my life more completely; it's been a long journey and one that's built over time. I believe being busy and finding the right people is paramount.

I'm currently working full-time and studying for my MBA. The best thing about the MBA is it gives me access to a network of high performers, people that are chasing the big goals in life and who are constantly challenging my understanding of what's possible. I love it.

If you're in rut, don't be afraid to get a new job, get a new something, get new people. People are the key to the next stage; once you know how you roll. And how you tap into your fire. The next thing to do is find people that also do this. Surround yourself with people you resonate with; it is just food for the soul.

Sometimes, if you're in a job where the people aren't your people, the only way to change the situation is to change the situation.

Your life is only a series of steps away from the life you want.

Step 1. It starts with understanding YOU.
Step 2. Surround yourself with people you want to be like or you can learn from.
Step 3. Make the necessary changes.
Step 4. Go forth and achieve.

11.6 There You Have It

So there you have it; my take on negotiating in the 21st century. I hope that through this book you have found some value to take your negotiations to the next level. It's been a journey and I thank you for coming on it with me. If you have questions or specific situations, then let's chat; don't be a stranger. Please give your review on Amazon, follow me on my Facebook page and get in touch and say hi via my website. I wish you all the success in the world with your negotiations. Go out there and make it happen. You only live on this Earth once; now is your time.

Website

www.tcastle.net

Facebook

@TimJSCastle

Amazon

If you have a moment, please can you give me a review on Amazon? It would mean the world to me and I'd be very grateful.

ACKNOWLEDGEMENTS

THERE ARE MANY people who have made this book possible and contributed in some way through their encouragement, teaching, mentorship and friendship.

Firstly, I would like to thank my partner, Sandra, for putting up with and tolerating my need to negotiate on practically everything from sofas to tuk tuks; thank you for believing in me.

Others who have a had a big direct and indirect influence on my life who I would like to thank are Mike Jenner, for teaching me the power of a world-class mindset, point of choice and turning insights into action; John Gibson, our form tutor of 7JG; thank you for pushing us to have the highest standards from the very beginning, for telling us the truth and setting us up for success; Sir Richard Branson, for showing me that business and fun should go together; Adam Grant for your books, Give and Take and Originals, and for engaging with me in words and wisdom when I reached out for advice; Linda Rysenbry for showing me a new approach to life and giving me the strength to change; To the team at Roma&Co in Manly for all those large lattes that kept me going and early 6am starts, you guys rock!

To Leila, John, Tim and the team at I AM Self-Publishing who have over delivered every single step of the way, you have been such a pleasure to work with and your skill and talent knows no bounds.

To my all my friends over the years, with a special mention to Richard Buckingham for suggesting I put pen to paper and write this book, and to Ryan Shorthouse, Marta Welander,

Chloe Turner and Corinna Henderson; your support and friendship means a lot.

Thanks to my parents, Robert and Anne Castle, for instilling in me that anything is possible and for supporting me wholeheartedly.

Finally, thanks to you the reader, for giving this book a go, for trying something new and putting you trust, money and time in me. Hopefully, you negotiated on the price. I'd be upset if you didn't.

Without you all it would not be possible and I sincerely thank you from the bottom of my heart.

RESOURCES

Blog Posts

https://www.linkedin.com/pulse/how-protect-yourself-against-selfish-people-adam-grant/

https://www.linkedin.com/pulse/20140515114346-69244073-if-you-do-this-your-emails-might-be-rude

Books

https://www.virgin.com/richard-branson/books/losing-my-virginity

https://www.amazon.com/Mental-Toughness-Secrets-World-Class/dp/0975500309

https://www.amazon.co.uk/Give-Take-Helping-Others-Success/dp/1780224729

https://www.principles.com/

http://dh.darrenhardy.com/tcebook

Videos

http://www.crocodileintheyangtze.com/

https://www.ted.com/talks/amy_cuddy_your_body_language_shapes_who_you_are

https://www.principles.com/#overlay

https://youtu.be/_rrcVEAfFHw

PDFs

https://hms.harvard.edu/sites/default/files/assets/Sites/
Ombuds/files/HMS.HHSD_.HSPH_.OmbudsOffice.
SEVEN%20ELEMENTS%20OF%20EFFECTIVE%20
NEGOTIATIONS.pdf

BIBLIOGRAPHY

O'Quin, K., Aronoff, J.: Humor as a technique of social influence. *Social Psychology Quarterly* 44(4), 349–357 (1981)

Brooks, A. W. 'Emotion and the Art of Negotiation'. *Harvard Business Review* 93(12) pp. 57-64. (2015)

http://bethanyhamilton.com/

Martin, R., A. *The Psychology of Humor: An Integrative Approach*, Elsevier Science, 2010

www.businessinsider.com.au/harvard-psychologist-amy-cuddy-how-people-judge-you-2016-1?r=US&IR=T

http://www.businessinsider.com.au/the-inspiring-life-story-of-alibaba-founder-jack-ma-2014-10#alibaba-employees-threw-a-big-party-at-the-companys-hangzhou-headquarters-to-celebrate-one-employee-even-took-the-party-as-the-perfect-opportunity-to-propose-ma-told-employees-at-a-press-conference-that-he-hopes-they-use-their-newfound-wealth-to-become-a-batch-of-genuinely-noble-people-a-batch-of-people-who-are-able-to-help-others-and-who-are-kind-and-happy-12

http://www.beliefnet.com/entertainment/sports/galleries/5-inspiring-athletes-who-overcame-disabilities.aspx?p=2

http://www.empowernet.com.au/blog/successful-people-who-faced-adversity/

https://hbr.org/2001/04/six-habits-of-merely-effective-negotiators

https://hbr.org/2010/03/the-art-of-the-cold-call-4-tip

https://hbr.org/2017/08/find-the-right-metrics-for-your-sales-team

https://www.linkedin.com/pulse/20130624114114-69244073-6-ways-to-get-me-to-email-you-back

https://www.linkedin.com/pulse/20140515114346-69244073-if-you-do-this-your-emails-might-be-rude

https://www.theguardian.com/technology/2016/nov/04/why-do-diplomats-use-this-alien-whatsapp-emoji-for-vladimir-putin?CMP=share_btn_fb

http://www.wired.co.uk/article/moty-cristal-negotiating-strategies

https://www.malwarebytes.com/

https://www.theguardian.com/technology/2016/aug/03/ransomware-threat-on-the-rise-as-40-of-businesses-attacked

http://www.wired.co.uk/article/cyber-attacks-hackers-ransoms

https://en.oxforddictionaries.com/word-of-the-year/word-of-the-year-2015

https://hbr.org/2014/04/15-rules-for-negotiating-a-job-offer

https://www.forbes.com/profile/jack-ma/

http://www.businessinsider.com/inspiring-life-story-of-alibaba-founder-jack-ma-2017-2/?r=AU&IR=T/#ma-has-largely-kept-his-family-life-out-of-the-spotlight-he-married-zhang-ying-a-teacher-whom-he-met-at-school-after-they-graduated-in-the-late-1980s-he-is-not-a-handsome-man-but-i-fell-for-him-because-he-can-do-a-lot-of-things-handsome-men-cannot-do-zhang-has-said-they-have-two-children-a-daughter-and-a-son-20

http://www.hnlr.org/2009/09/power-and-trust-in-negotiation-and-decision-making-a-critical-evaluation/

https://www.negotiationtraining.com.au/articles/next-best-option/

https://www.pon.harvard.edu/daily/batna/translate-your-batna-to-the-current-deal/

Printed in Great Britain
by Amazon